Frommer's®

Yosemite and Sequoia & Kings Canyon National Parks

7th Edition

by Eric Peterson

WILEY

Wiley Publishing, Inc.

Published by:

WILEY PUBLISHING, INC.

111 River St.
Hoboken, NJ 07030-5774

ISBN 978-0-470-53773-2

Editor: Leslie A. Shen
Production Editor: Erin Amick
Cartographer: Nick Trotter
Photo Editor: Richard Fox
Production by Wiley Indianapolis Composition Services

Front cover photo: Lembert Dome and the Tuolumne River, Yosemite
National Park, California. © Russ Bishop/Alamy Images

For information on our other products and services or to obtain technical
support, please contact our Customer Care Department within the U.S. at
877/762-2974, outside the U.S. at 317/572-3993 or fax 317/572-4002.

Wiley also publishes its books in a variety of electronic formats. Some con-
tent that appears in print may not be available in electronic formats.

Manufactured in the United States of America

5   4   3   2   1

CONTENTS

LIST OF MAPS

ABOUT THE AUTHOR

A Denver-based freelance writer, **Eric Peterson** has contributed to numerous Frommer's guides covering the American West, and has written *Frommer's Montana & Wyoming, Frommer's Colorado, Frommer's Yellowstone & Grand Teton National Parks,* and *Ramble: A Field Guide to the U.S.A.* Peterson also writes about travel and other topics for such publications as *ColoradoBiz, Delta Sky,* and the *New York Daily News.* In his free time, he's an avid camper and hiker, a lifelong Broncos fan, and a part-time rock star (at least in the eyes of his niece Olivia and nephews Mitch and Sam).

HOW TO CONTACT US

In researching this book, we discovered many wonderful places—hotels, restaurants, shops, and more. We're sure you'll find others. Please tell us about them, so we can share the information with your fellow travelers in upcoming editions. If you were disappointed with a recommendation, we'd love to know that, too. Please write to:

Frommer's Yosemite and Sequoia & Kings Canyon National Parks, 7th Edition
Wiley Publishing, Inc. • 111 River St. • Hoboken, NJ 07030-5774

AN ADDITIONAL NOTE

FROMMER'S STAR RATINGS, ICONS & ABBREVIATIONS

Every hotel, restaurant, and attraction listing in this guide has been ranked for quality, value, service, amenities, and special features using a **star-rating system.** In country, state, and regional guides, we also rate towns and regions to help you narrow down your choices and budget your time accordingly. Hotels and restaurants are rated on a scale of zero (recommended) to three stars (exceptional). Attractions, shopping, nightlife, towns, and regions are rated according to the following scale: zero stars (recommended), one star (highly recommended), two stars (very highly recommended), and three stars (must-see).

In addition to the star-rating system, we also use **seven feature icons** that point you to the great deals, in-the-know advice, and unique experiences that separate travelers from tourists. Throughout the book, look for:

Finds	Special finds—those places only insiders know about
Fun Facts	Fun facts—details that make travelers more informed and their trips more fun
Kids	Best bets for kids, and advice for the whole family
Moments	Special moments—those experiences that memories are made of
Overrated	Places or experiences not worth your time or money
Tips	Insider tips—great ways to save time and money
Value	Great values—where to get the best deals

The following **abbreviations** are used for credit cards:

AE	American Express	**DISC**	Discover	**V**	Visa
DC	Diners Club	**MC**	MasterCard		

TRAVEL RESOURCES AT FROMMERS.COM

Frommer's travel resources don't end with this guide. Frommer's website, **www.frommers.com**, has travel information on more than 4,000 destinations. We update features regularly, giving you access to the most current trip-planning information and the best airfare, lodging, and car-rental bargains. You can also listen to podcasts, connect with other Frommers.com members through our active-reader forums, share your travel photos, read blogs from guidebook editors and fellow travelers, and much more.

Introduction to Yosemite and Sequoia & Kings Canyon National Parks

California's Sierra Nevada imposes rugged features on a state that many associate with sandy beaches and palm trees. It's a mountain range of great beauty, hidden amid harsh wilderness, and nowhere is the terrain more dramatic than in Yosemite and Sequoia & Kings Canyon National Parks. These truly special places combine mountains with meadows, waterfalls with wildflowers, and spectacular geology with awe-inspiring vistas that span, in some cases, nearly the breadth of the state. Together, the parks cover 1.6 million acres (roughly 2,500 sq. miles). They host over four million visitors a year and are home to thousands of species of plants and animals.

Yosemite attracts more tourists than Sequoia & Kings Canyon combined, although all three are absolutely delightful parks. Yosemite covers 1,169 square miles—roughly the size of Rhode Island—and 94% is designated wilderness. Here you can enjoy the quiet beauty of a forest or a pristine meadow, observe a sunset from a towering granite cliff, hike a half-mile-high waterfall, enjoy a moonlit night that's as bright as day, climb a world-famous rock, and eat a gourmet meal before falling asleep—be it under the stars or in the luxurious bed of a top-rated hotel.

Yosemite Valley, which attracts 95% of all Yosemite tourists, is just 1% of the park by area, but contains a number of the region's jaw-dropping features, and is visited by over three million people each year. It's a place of record-setting statistics, too: The highest waterfall in North America and three of the tallest in the world (Upper Yosemite, Sentinel, and Ribbon falls), as well as the biggest and tallest piece of exposed granite (El Capitan), are here.

Wawona, a small community annexed to the park in 1932, is a 45-minute drive south of Yosemite Valley. Mostly a hodgepodge of resort cabins and private homes, Wawona is also home to the stately Wawona Hotel, a 9-hole golf course, and a main attraction—the

Sequoia & Kings Canyon National Parks

1

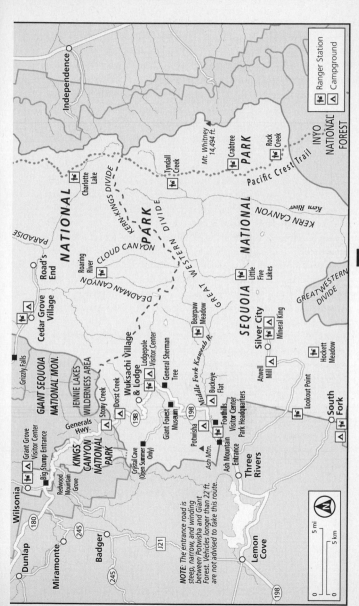

NOTE: The entrance road is steep, narrow, and winding between Potwisha and Giant Forest. Vehicles longer than 22 ft. are not advised to take this route.

Mariposa Grove, the largest grove of giant sequoias in Yosemite. There are two smaller groves located near Crane Flat, about a half-hour drive west of Yosemite Valley.

Yosemite National Park's Tuolumne Meadows (an immense plateau peppered with wildflowers during the summer) and the glimmering Tuolumne River are a 1½-hour drive northeast of the valley. Tuolumne Meadows is surrounded by a half-dozen domes and peaks. The high country also includes Tenaya Lake, White Wolf Lodge, and Tuolumne Meadows Lodge, though the two lodges are little more than restaurants with a collection of tent-cabins. These accommodations, plus backcountry outposts accessible only on foot, are described in chapter 5, "Where to Stay & Eat in Yosemite."

In the heart of the Sierra Nevada, just south of Yosemite, are Sequoia & Kings Canyon National Parks, home to both the largest giant sequoia trees in the world and a deep gorge of a canyon that rivals Yosemite Valley for awe-inspiring beauty. Sequoia & Kings Canyon are separate parks snuggled next to each other and managed jointly. Combined, they outsize Yosemite. Peaks stretch across 1,350 square miles and include 14,505-foot Mount Whitney, the tallest point in the lower 48 states. These parks are also home to the Kaweah Range, a string of stark and magnificently beautiful mountains nestled among the Sierra. Three powerful rivers, the Kings, Kern, and Kaweah, tumble through the parks. Despite their large size, Sequoia & Kings Canyon National Parks attract less than half the number of Yosemite's annual visitors, making them a great alternative for those looking to avoid huge crowds.

1 HISTORY OF THE REGION

This region of the Sierra Nevada has a rich natural and cultural history. The landscape can change completely from one mile to the next. High mountain meadows give way to turbulent rivers that thunder down deep gorges, tumble over vast waterfalls, and turn into wide, shallow rivers as they meander through the next valley. Such diversity can be attributed to the region's geologic roots, which stretch back 10 to 80 million years when a head-on collision between two immense plates of rock formed this mountain range. The rock, weakened by extreme temperature variations, was later carved by erosion into deep valleys, including Yosemite Valley and Kings Canyon. In a process described more fully in chapter 9, "A Nature Guide to Yosemite and Sequoia & Kings Canyon National Parks," the Ice Age brought glaciers that smoothed the faces of rocks such as Yosemite's El Capitan and Half Dome, some of the towering peaks of Yosemite's Tuolumne Meadows, and Kings Canyon itself.

American Indians were aware of Yosemite at least 5,000 years ago. While Egyptian scholars were making their first use of numbers, American Indians in California were living as their forebears had for thousands of years. By 1000 B.C., there were tribes—including the Ahwahneeches (Ah-*wah*-nee-ches), a subtribe of the Miwok—living in Yosemite Valley. Archaeologists have since documented 36 living sites on the valley floor that supported a vast number of inhabitants with lush vegetation and numerous animals. The largest village lay just below Yosemite Falls.

Despite the fact that the early inhabitants were called Ahwahneeches, the valley was named Yosemite by soldiers sent to oust American Indians who refused to relocate to the plains. While seated around a campfire, a doctor among the group suggested the soldiers settle on a name for the valley. Among the suggestions were Paradise Valley and Yosemite, the name by which the Indian tribes in the region were known. Some were offended by the suggestion of honoring American Indians in the valley, but in the end, the name Yosemite won. Ironically, however, Yosemite was the soldiers' mispronunciation of the word Oo-*hoo*-ma-te, the name of just one settlement of Ahwahneeches, whom soldiers drove from Yosemite Valley in 1851.

The Ahwahneeches' neighbors, the Monaches (also known as the Western Monos), lived in Kings Canyon and met their end during a smallpox outbreak in 1862. The Monaches kept villages in the foothills all year long, although they sometimes moved to the forest in the summer. The Potwishas and Wuksachis were sub-tribes of the Monaches who also lived in the foothills, around Sequoia's Ash Mountain. Kings Canyon was named in 1806 by the Spaniard Gabriel Moraga, the first European to lead an expedition in these parts. Moraga's party discovered a major river on January 6, the Roman Catholic day of the Epiphany. Being a good Catholic, Moraga christened the river El Río de los Santos Reyes, or "the river of the holy kings," in honor of the three wise men who visited the infant Jesus on the same date, albeit many years earlier. The name was later shortened to Kings River.

The land of Kings Canyon and Sequoia remained untouched until 1827, when trappers arrived. The California gold rush drew hordes more in 1849, and abandoned mines dot Sequoia & Kings Canyon National Parks, especially in Mineral King, a region unsuccessfully mined for silver in the 1800s.

Despite being plagued by natural upheavals, such as prehistoric earthquakes and glaciers, Yosemite, Sequoia, and Kings Canyon survived. Then the parks faced another challenge—each was destined for

Impressions

The clearest way into the Universe is through a forest wilderness.
—Author and naturalist John Muir

destruction by dams, logging, and consequent flooding. Large stands of giant sequoia were obliterated in the late 1800s. Ranchers allowed their sheep to graze beneath the big trees. Sawmills were built, and zip-zip—down came entire forests. Adding insult to injury is the fact that the wood of the largest giant sequoias is brittle and generally pretty useless. Nevertheless, early loggers chopped down a third of the ancient trees in the region. This travesty would likely have continued if not for a few mid-19th-century conservationists, who pushed the government to turn the areas into parks. In 1890, Sequoia National Park was created, along with the tiny General Grant National Park, established to protect Grant Grove. Unfortunately, the move came too late to spare Converse Basin. Once the largest stand of giant sequoias in the world, today it's a cemetery of tree stumps, the grave markers of fallen giants.

In 1926, the park was expanded eastward to include the small Kern Canyon and Mount Whitney, but rumblings continued over the fate of Kings Canyon itself. For a while, its future lay as a reservoir. It wasn't until the 1960s that Kings Canyon was finally protected for good. In 1978, Mineral King was added to Sequoia's half of the park, and in 2001, President Bill Clinton established Giant Sequoia National Monument in the national forest adjacent to the parks. The parks have been managed jointly since World War II.

While the fight to save the giant sequoias raged, a similar battle was taking place over Yosemite. Here the threat came from opportunists hoping to cash in on Yosemite Valley's beauty. Soon after the Ahwah-neeches were driven out, homesteaders came in. They built hotels and crude homes and planted row crops and orchards. Somehow, during the Civil War, Congress convinced President Abraham Lincoln to sign legislation protecting the valley and the nearby Mariposa Grove of giant sequoias. Yosemite Valley was, in effect, the first state and national park in America. But the thousands of acres surrounding these relatively small federal holdings were still subject to exploitation in the form of mining, logging, and grazing. Happily, on October 1, 1890, a week after approving Sequoia National Park, Congress estab-lished Yosemite National Park. The new park did not include the valley or Mariposa Grove, which were still part of the older Yosemite

Valley Park, but it encompassed enormous tracts of surrounding wilderness. With two administrations—one overseeing the valley and big trees, and one overseeing the new park—the expected overlap occurred and frustration mounted. In 1906, legislators decided to add the valley and big trees to the new park and to reduce the park's size to follow the natural contours of the land, while excluding private mining and logging operations. Everyone was set to live happily ever after. No one would have predicted that Yosemite would become one of the most popular places on the planet. (Though some argue that tourism has accomplished the destruction that logging couldn't.)

Recent years have brought more and more human activity to this wilderness haven. Today, this is the biggest challenge facing Yosemite and, to a lesser extent, Sequoia & Kings Canyon. Big changes are expected as the National Park Service grapples with the best way to permit access without causing more irreparable damage to this natural wonderland.

Who would have thought that preservation would wreak its own brand of havoc here? But we can only imagine how this beautiful place would look today had it been left in the hands of profiteers.

2 THE PARKS TODAY

More than three million people visit Yosemite annually. In the summer, the average daily census hits 20,000! The major difficulty facing park officials today, due to the park's increasing popularity, is balancing humanity's access to Yosemite's wonders with the need to maintain and improve the park's health. The National Park Service issued a master plan in 2000, aimed at reducing vehicle traffic in Yosemite Valley. Parts of this plan have already been put into effect, and additional changes are planned that will somewhat limit access, especially personal vehicle access, to the park. Many who love Yosemite say this is a small price to pay to protect a treasure.

It's a far different scenario at Sequoia & Kings Canyon National Parks. They get crowded in summer, too, when RVs and slow drivers can form convoys dozens of cars long—but it's nothing like Yosemite. Sequoia & Kings Canyon are much less developed, and the spots that are developed are much more spread out. Frankly, officials here learned a lesson from Yosemite and worked hard not to make the same mistakes. The park is awe-inspiring, with voluptuous canyons and some of the most spectacular trees and vistas in the Sierra, but they are not all crammed into a 7-mile valley, and you won't find a crowd three deep jostling for a view, as in Yosemite.

Crowds aside, there's a movement at both Yosemite and Sequoia & Kings Canyon to return the parks to a more natural state. Nowhere is this more evident than in Yosemite Valley, where nature is forcing officials to make changes long planned but never implemented. For more than 20 years, Yosemite National Park was governed in part by a general plan that called for restoring meadows, phasing out some campgrounds, and moving others away from waterways to reduce the human impact on rivers, streams, and wildlife. However, little progress had been made.

Then in January 1997, a torrential downpour turned into one of the most destructive winter storms on record, and when the rain stopped several days later, Yosemite Valley was Yosemite Lake. Swollen streams and creeks swept tons of debris—trees, rocks, brush—into the valley, clogging the Merced River. Campgrounds were submerged, employees' quarters were flooded, and much of Yosemite Lodge was under 2 feet of water. Despite frantic attempts at sandbagging, hundreds of people were forced onto higher ground—the top floors of buildings—and everyone was stuck. The water was so high and so ferocious that it washed out the roads and stranded about 2,000 people in the valley. So much was damaged that the valley closed for almost 3 months, and, even after it was reopened, travel was restricted for several months to the park's all-weather highway. In 1997, a decision was made to reconsider rebuilding the hundreds of lost campsites. And, since 2001, litigation has held up pretty much any and all construction and reconstruction projects in Yosemite Valley (though a 2007 ruling allowed the park service to undertake "critical" projects such as repaving roads).

The storms remind us of the history behind these parks. Millions of years of water, snow, and glaciers carved the unique gorges of Yosemite Valley and Kings Canyon. So the folks who live here do so with a measure of understanding: They're living at the mercy of nature.

But the post-flood political battle highlights the Park Service's difficult dual mission: to not only conserve wilderness, but also allow recreational access. In this context, park management's reconstruction plans must walk a very fine line—and rarely is everybody happy, if ever.

In Sequoia & Kings Canyon, park officials have a 16-year sequoia forest restoration project under their belts at Giant Forest, where old buildings were torn down and roads and parking lots moved in an effort to return this area of the park to a more natural state. The goal is ecological restoration—to cease damaging the sequoias' root systems, repair the topsoil, plant sequoia seedlings, and get out of the way while Mother Nature does her thing. An added benefit is that without the buildings, this area is now more attractive.

Interestingly, park officials also hope that natural fires will return to the area once the heavy human impact is reduced. Fires are an important part of the sequoia's life. The bark of the giant trees is fire resistant, but a blaze will dry out the sequoia's cones. The dried cones then open, dropping seeds onto the fire-cleared ground, which is, conveniently, the preferred growth medium for seedlings.

3 THE BEST OF YOSEMITE AND SEQUOIA & KINGS CANYON

It's hard to pick the best of anything, and it's especially difficult to declare something "best" when nature is involved. There are so many heart-thumping hikes, roaring waterfalls, and mind-blowing vistas to explore in these parks that it's almost impossible to pick our favorites. That being said, we're ready with a few suggestions.

THE BEST VIEWS

- **The Panorama from Tunnel View Outside Yosemite Valley:** If you're approaching the park on CA 41 from Wawona, this amazing panorama will sneak up on you, offering a breathtaking surprise. There's plenty of space in the two parking lots to pull over and look. See "South of the Valley" in the "Orientation" section of chapter 3.
- **Yosemite Valley from Glacier Point:** The easy drive to the top of Glacier Point (open in summer only) will leave you speechless. From here, you'll get an eye-level view of the great rocks, such as Half Dome, North Dome, and Cloud's Rest. The stunning valley and waterfalls are spread far below. See chapter 3.
- **Mist Falls from the Bottom in Kings Canyon:** Standing at the base of this waterfall, you'll really appreciate its force, especially during spring and early summer when it's fed by the snowmelt. The crashing of water onto the rocks below drowns out all other noise, and there are rainbows galore. Keep back from the slippery rocks at its edge! See chapters 6 and 7.

THE BEST CAR CAMPGROUNDS

- **North Pines Campground in Yosemite Valley:** Smaller and slightly more isolated than neighboring campgrounds, North Pines offers a true forest camping experience that makes it the most enjoyable of Yosemite Valley's car campgrounds. See p. 80.

- **Buckeye Flat Campground in Sequoia:** This is a small, secluded, and especially pretty campground in the Foothills area, with a prime location amid a grove of oaks. The only downfall is that it can get very hot in the summer. See p. 133.
- **Sunset Campground in Kings Canyon:** Spread over a rolling hilltop beneath tall trees, this is a peaceful place that glows late into the evening as the sun goes down. It offers some nicely secluded sites, and it's well located for hikes to some of the park's most impressive big trees. See p. 133.

THE BEST PRIMITIVE CAMPGROUNDS

- **Yosemite Creek Campground:** Just outside Yosemite Valley on CA 120, you'll find this great out-of-the-way campground. It lacks amenities, but is far enough off the beaten path to offer solitude. Few venture down the 5-mile dirt road to this campground, but those who do tend to prefer roughing it. See p. 81.
- **South Fork Campground in Sequoia:** This is the smallest developed campsite in the park. It's just inside the park's boundary, set at 3,650 feet along the South Fork of the beautiful Kaweah River. See p. 133.
- **Atwell Mill Campground in Sequoia:** The site is situated along Atwell Creek near the East Fork of the Kaweah River in the Mineral King region of the park. You'll need time and patience to reach it—allow at least an hour for the 20-mile drive—but it's well worth it. See p. 133.

THE BEST DAY HIKES

- **Vernal Fall in Yosemite:** A must-see for anyone with the stamina. It's just 3 miles round-trip if you follow the Mist Trail, but it requires a strong heart and enough gumption to make the last quarter-mile, ascending 500 stairs. Once at the top, hikers are rewarded with fabulous views and enough space to lounge around like marmots in the sun before the hike back down. See p. 52.
- **Moro Rock in Sequoia:** A short but steep climb up a historic staircase that snakes through rock crevices to the top of Moro Rock. Rewards include one of the most awe-inspiring views in the Sierra Nevada. The walk offers plenty of places to rest on the way up. See p. 113.
- **Mist Falls in Kings Canyon:** This 8-mile round-trip hike climbs 1,500 feet to the spectacular Mist Falls. Along the way, the hiking ranges from moderately strenuous to easy strolling through woodland areas that have lots of places where you can catch your breath. See p. 117.

THE BEST HIGH-COUNTRY HIKES

- **May Lake in Yosemite:** This is an easy 2.5-mile hike that begins near Tioga Road, east of White Wolf (accessible by motor vehicle in summer only). The picturesque walk offers fishing, but no swimming. May Lake is dead center in Yosemite National Park. It's a good place to survey the surrounding peaks, including the 10,855-foot-high Mount Hoffman rising behind the lake. See p. 57.

- **The High Sierra Trail in Sequoia:** This popular backpacking trail offers day hikers a glimpse of what's out there. It's a moderate, 10-mile hike with pretty views of the Middle Fork of the Kaweah River and the Kaweah Range. See p. 123.

- **Paradise Valley in Kings Canyon:** This hike extends beyond Mist Falls to a broad valley bisected by a welcoming river. The long 14-mile round-trip hike is a bit much to do in 1 day, but it is possible with some planning and an early start. See p. 118.

THE BEST MEALS

- **The Ahwahnee Dining Room in Yosemite Valley:** No surprise here—it's a knockout feast. Every course is almost worth its weight in gold, which is about what it'll cost you, too. See p. 86.

- **Mountain Room Restaurant in Yosemite Valley:** Some people like the Mountain Room even better than the top-rated Ahwahnee. Not only is the food here top-notch, but you also can't beat the views of Yosemite Falls. See p. 88.

- **Wawona Dining Room in Yosemite:** Located outside the valley, this spacious hotel restaurant is a favorite of locals for miles around. The excellent chef concocts delectable meals, and the views through the expanse of windows provide food for the soul. See p. 89.

THE BEST PLACES FOR REFLECTION

- **Yosemite's Glacier Point at Night:** You're sure to be quietly overwhelmed, either by the number of stars or the way the moonlight reflects off the granite domes surrounding the valley. See chapters 3 and 4.

- **Tenaya Lake in Yosemite:** The solitude and beauty of this high-altitude, crystal-clear lake (accessible by road in summer only) outshines others in the park. Tenaya Lake is larger and more dramatic, edging up against an iridescent granite landscape. See chapters 3 and 4.

- **The Backcountry:** Yosemite and Sequoia & Kings Canyon offer great backcountry getaways. Modern backpacking was invented in the Sierra Nevada and remains one of the cornerstone recreational activities in the summertime here. Few places are as well suited for contemplation as a trail into the wilds. See chapters 4 and 7.

Planning Your Trip to Yosemite and Sequoia & Kings Canyon National Parks

In the pages that follow, you'll find all the information you need before setting off on your adventure to one of these spectacular national parks.

1 WHEN TO GO

Both Yosemite and Sequoia & Kings Canyon are open year-round.

YOSEMITE   Avoid holiday weekends in spring and summer if possible—park campgrounds are usually full June through August—and expect some crowds in late spring and early fall as well. Winter is a great time to visit Yosemite: Not only is the park virtually empty, but there are also a number of winter-only activities, from cross-country skiing, snowshoeing, and ice skating to downhill skiing and sledding at Badger Pass. Keep in mind that the high country along Tioga and Glacier Point roads is inaccessible to motor vehicles from mid-fall to early June, when deep snow closes the roads.

SEQUOIA & KINGS CANYON   Like Yosemite, a variety of attractions stay open at these parks all year, but Cedar Grove is closed from mid-November to mid-April and Mineral King is closed from November 1 until Memorial Day weekend. Summertime sees a lively population of adventure seekers (see chapter 7, "Hikes & Other Outdoor Pursuits in Sequoia & Kings Canyon"). Note that the hiking-trail passes in the high country may be snowbound until July.

CLIMATE

The climate at both Yosemite and Sequoia & Kings Canyon varies considerably, depending on the region of the park. A good rule of thumb is to remember that the higher you go, the cooler it gets. So pack a parka on any trip that climbs above the valley floor or ventures into the backcountry.

In summer, Fahrenheit temperatures at lower elevations (such as Yosemite Valley) can climb into the 90s (30s Celsius) and higher, and plummet into the 50s (10s Celsius) at night. Afternoon temperatures average in the 60s and 70s (10s–20s Celsius) in spring and fall, and again, evenings are usually cool. Afternoon showers are fairly common fall through spring. Winter days average in the 40s and 50s (5–10s Celsius), and it seldom drops below 0°F (-18°C), although much of the land above 5,500 feet is buried beneath several feet of snow.

The high country gets up to 20 feet of snow half the year, so visitors should be experienced in winter travel. November through March, it is wise to expect snow and be prepared. Remember, particularly wet winters lead to incredibly stunning and powerful spring waterfalls, especially in Yosemite.

SPECIAL EVENTS IN YOSEMITE

JANUARY TO FEBRUARY

Chefs' Holidays. Yosemite hosts nationally renowned chefs who share their culinary secrets with participants. Packages that include accommodations at the Ahwahnee are available. Call © **801/559-5000** for reservations.

MARCH

Heritage Holidays. Started in 2002 to celebrate the Ahwahnee's 75th birthday, this is a nostalgic treat for visitors, with many events—concerts, lectures, and movies—free and open to the public. Lodging packages at the Ahwahnee and the Yosemite Lodge at the Falls are available. Call © **801/559-5000** for more information.

NOVEMBER TO DECEMBER

Vintners' Holidays. California's finest winemakers hold tastings in the Ahwahnee's Great Lounge. Each session concludes with a Vintners' Banquet. The four-course gala event, held in the Ahwahnee Dining Room, pairs four wines with specially selected food. Two- and 3-night packages are available. Call © **801/559-5000** for reservations.

DECEMBER

The Bracebridge Dinner ★★. Held on 8 evenings from December 15 to the day after Christmas, this event transports diners to 17th-century England, with music, food, and song. The festivities take place in the Ahwahnee Dining Room, bedecked with wreaths, banners, and traditional yuletide decorations. This popular event requires reservations, which are secured by lottery. Applications are available from December 1 to January 15 and are due February 15 for the coming year. Prices change from year to year, but expect to pay around $500 per person. Call $\textcircled{C}$ **801/559-5000** for more information.

SPECIAL EVENTS IN SEQUOIA & KINGS CANYON

SEPTEMBER

Celebrate Sequoias Festival. Kings Canyon National Park hosts this annual event on the first Saturday of September after Labor Day. This all-day event includes walks to lesser-known sequoia groves, living-history presentations, botanists' talks, children's activities, and an arts-and-crafts fair. Call $\textcircled{C}$ **559/565-3341** for more information.

DECEMBER

Trek to the Tree ★★★. This annual tradition, on the second Sunday in December at 2:30pm, is the main event at Kings Canyon. The Christmas ceremony takes place at the General Grant Tree and includes a solemn and moving tribute to Americans who have given their lives in service to their country. Former parks superintendent Col. John White said it best: "We are gathered here around a tree that is worthy of representing the spirit of America on Christmas Day. That spirit is best expressed in the plain things of life, the love of the family circle, the simple life of the out-of-doors. The tree is a pillar that is a testimony that things of the spirit transcend those of the flesh." The event is organized by the **Sanger District Chamber of Commerce** ($\textcircled{C}$ **559/875-4575;** www.sanger.org).

2 ENTRY REQUIREMENTS

PASSPORTS

Virtually every air traveler entering the U.S. is required to show a passport. All persons, including U.S. citizens, traveling by air between the United States and Canada, Mexico, Central and South America, the Caribbean, and Bermuda are required to present a valid passport. U.S. and Canadian citizens entering the U.S. at land and sea ports of entry from within the Western Hemisphere will need to present government-issued proof of citizenship, such as a birth certificate, along with a government-issued photo ID, such as a driver's license. A passport is not required for U.S. or Canadian citizens entering by land or sea, but carrying one is highly encouraged.

VISAS

Citizens of certain countries are required to have a visa to travel to the U.S. For information on obtaining a visa, please see chapter 10, "Fast Facts."

The U.S. State Department has a **Visa Waiver Program (VWP)** allowing citizens of the following countries to enter the United States without a visa for stays of up to 90 days: Andorra, Australia, Austria, Belgium, Brunei, Denmark, Finland, France, Germany, Iceland, Ireland, Italy, Japan, Liechtenstein, Luxembourg, Monaco, the Netherlands, New Zealand, Norway, Portugal, San Marino, Singapore, Slovenia, Spain, Sweden, Switzerland, and the United Kingdom. Citizens of Czech Republic, Estonia, Hungary, Latvia, Lithuania, Malta, Republic of Korea, and Slovakia are soon to be admitted to the VWP. (*Note:* This list was accurate at press time; for the most up-to-date list of countries in the VWP, consult http://travel.state.gov/visa.) Even though a visa isn't necessary, in an effort to help U.S. officials check travelers against terror watch lists before they arrive at U.S. borders, visitors from VWP countries must register online through the Electronic System for Travel Authorization (ESTA) before boarding a plane or a boat to the U.S. Travelers will complete an electronic application providing basic personal and travel eligibility information. The Department of Homeland Security recommends filling out the form at least 3 days before traveling. Authorizations will be valid for up to 2 years or until the traveler's passport expires, whichever comes first. Currently, there is no fee for the online application. *Note:* Any passport issued on or after October 26, 2006, by a VWP country must be an **e-Passport** for VWP travelers to be eligible to enter the U.S. without a visa. Citizens of these nations also need to present a round-trip air or cruise ticket upon arrival. E-Passports contain computer chips capable of storing biometric information, such as the required digital photograph of the holder. If your passport doesn't have this feature, you can still travel without a visa if it is a valid passport issued before October 26, 2005, and includes a machine-readable zone, or between October 26, 2005, and October 25, 2006, and includes a digital photograph. For more information, go to **http://travel.state.gov/visa**. Canadian citizens may enter the United

States without visas; however, they will need to show passports (if traveling by air) and proof of residence.

Citizens of all other countries must have (1) a valid passport that expires at least 6 months later than the scheduled end of their visit to the U.S., and (2) a tourist visa.

---

3 GETTING THERE & GETTING AROUND

GETTING TO YOSEMITE NATIONAL PARK
By Plane
Fresno Yosemite International Airport (© 559/621-4500), located 90 miles from Yosemite National Park's South Entrance at Wawona, is the nearest major airport, serving over 25 cities with more than 100 flights daily. **Alaska Airlines/Horizon Air** (www.alaskaair.com), **Allegiant Air** (www.allegiantair.com), **American Airlines** (www.aa.com), **Delta Air Lines** (www.delta.com), **Great Lakes Airlines** (www.flygreatlakes.com), **Mexicana Airlines** (www.mexicana.com), **United** (www.united.com), and **US Airways** (www.usairways.com) all service Fresno airport.

By Car
Yosemite is a 3½-hour drive from San Francisco and a 6-hour drive from Los Angeles. Many roads lead to Yosemite's four entrances. From the west, the Big Oak Flat Entrance is 88 miles from Manteca via CA 120, which passes through the towns of Groveland, Buck Meadows, and Big Oak Flat. The Arch Rock Entrance is 75 miles northeast of Merced via CA 140, which passes through Mariposa and El Portal. The South Entrance is 64 miles north of Fresno and passes through Oakhurst, Bass Lake, and Fish Camp. From the east, the Tioga Pass Entrance is the only option; it's 10 miles west of Lee Vining via CA 120, although this route is usually open only in the summer. To check on statewide road conditions, call © 800/427-7623 in California (© 916/445-7623 outside of the state) or visit **www.dot.ca.gov**.

Although not available within the national parks, most of the major car-rental companies can be found in Fresno, including **Advantage** (www.advantage.com), **Alamo** (www.alamo.com), **Avis** (www.avis.com), **Budget** (www.budget.com), **Dollar** (www.dollar.com), **Enterprise** (www.enterprise.com), **Hertz** (www.hertz.com), **National** (www.nationalcar.com), **Payless** (www.paylesscarrental.com), and **Thrifty** (www.thrifty.com).

International visitors should note that insurance and taxes are almost never included in quoted rental-car rates in the U.S. Be sure to ask your rental agency about additional fees for these. They can add a significant cost to your car rental.

By Bus

Daily bus transportation into the park from Merced, Mariposa, and other nearby communities is provided by the **Yosemite Area Regional Transportation System,** or **YARTS** (© 877/989-2787 or 209/388-9589; www.yarts.com). Buses are not subject to park entrance delays during peak season. From Merced, there are several YARTS departures daily from the airport, the Amtrak train station, and the Greyhound bus terminal. Round-trip fare is $25 for adults, $18 for children 12 and under and seniors 62 and older. There are stops in Mariposa at several lodgings and the visitor center, with round-trip rates of $12 for adults and $8 for children and seniors.

Greyhound (© 800/231-2222; www.greyhound.com) also links Merced with many other California cities.

By Train

Amtrak (© 800/872-7245; www.amtrak.com) serves Fresno and Merced on its San Joaquin route.

GETTING TO SEQUOIA & KINGS CANYON NATIONAL PARKS

By Plane

Fresno Yosemite International Airport (© 559/621-4500) is the nearest major airport, located 53 miles from the Big Stump Entrance of Kings Canyon. See the section on Yosemite, above, to find out which airlines service Fresno.

Visalia Municipal Airport (© 559/713-4201; www.flyvisalia. com), 36 miles from the Ash Mountain Entrance, is served by **Great Lakes Airlines** (© 800/554-5111), with daily flights to Ontario International Airport near Los Angeles.

By Car

There are two entrances to the parks. CA 198 east, via Visalia and the town of Three Rivers, leads to the Ash Mountain Entrance in Sequoia National Park, while CA 180 east, via Fresno, leads straight to the Big Stump Entrance near Grant Grove in Kings Canyon National Park. Both entrances are approximately 4 hours from Los Angeles and 5 hours from San Francisco. To check on statewide road conditions, call © 800/427-7623 in California (© 916/445-7623 outside of the state) or visit **www.dot.ca.gov**. For rental-car information, see the section on Yosemite, above.

By Bus

Greyhound (© 800/231-2222) serves Visalia and Fresno. In Sequoia & Kings Canyon, the **Sequoia Shuttle** (© 877/287-4453; www.sequoiashuttle.com) connects Visalia with the Giant Forest area of the park; it runs in summer for $10 per person.

By Train

Amtrak (© 800/872-7245; www.amtrak.com) serves Fresno and Merced on its San Joaquin route and connects Visalia with the Hanford station via bus service.

GETTING AROUND YOSEMITE AND SEQUOIA & KINGS CANYON

By Car

The most popular way to get around the parks is by car. It follows that in peak season, the roads can get swamped with traffic, hitting its zenith around 3 or 4pm in the afternoon. Trips including both Yosemite and Sequoia & Kings Canyon nearly demand a car to get between the two areas.

By Bus

Daily bus transportation into Yosemite is provided by the **Yosemite Area Regional Transportation System,** or **YARTS** (© **877/989-2787** or 209/388-9589; www.yarts.com). Buses are not subject to park entrance delays during peak season.

Within Yosemite National Park, there are free **shuttles** in Yosemite Valley, Tuolumne Meadows, and Wawona, and a free bus between Wawona and the valley in summer and between the valley and Badger Pass in winter. For a fee, there are also buses between Tuolumne Meadows and the valley and between the valley and Glacier Point.

In Sequoia & Kings Canyon, the **Sequoia Shuttle** (© **877/287-4453;** www.sequoiashuttle.com) connects Visalia with the Giant Forest area; it runs in summer for $10 per person. A free in-park **shuttle** takes visitors from Giant Forest to Lodgepole, Moro Rock, and other destinations.

4 MONEY & COSTS

The Value of U.S. Dollars vs. Other Popular Currencies

US$	Can$	UK£	Euro (€)	Aus$	NZ$
$1.00	C$1.09	£0.61	€0.70	A$1.19	NZ$1.47

Frommer's lists exact prices in the local currency. The currency conversions quoted above were correct at press time. However, rates fluctuate, so before departing consult a currency-exchange website such as **www.oanda.com/convert/classic** to check up-to-the-minute rates.

Yosemite is a premium-priced destination, with lodging and meals priced accordingly high, especially during the summer season. In fall and spring, room rates drop precipitously. Sequoia & Kings Canyon are more moderately priced. There are ATMs in most of the developed areas in all of the parks.

5 HEALTH

STAYING HEALTHY

Health hazards range from mild headaches to run-ins with wild animals, but the latter happen less frequently than car accidents in the parks. To be on the safe side, you might want to keep a **first-aid kit** in your car or luggage, and have it handy when hiking. It should include, at the least, butterfly bandages, sterile gauze pads, adhesive tape, an antibiotic ointment, pain relievers for both children and adults, alcohol pads, a pocketknife with scissors, and tweezers.

COMMON AILMENTS

ALTITUDE SICKNESS The most common health hazard is the discomfort felt as visitors adjust to the parks' high elevations. Altitude sickness is a process that can take a day or more. Symptoms include headache, fatigue, nausea, loss of appetite, muscle pain, and light-headedness. Doctors recommend that, until acclimated, travelers should avoid heavy exertion, consume light meals, and drink lots of liquids, avoiding those with caffeine or alcohol.

BUGS, BITES & OTHER WILDLIFE CONCERNS Wildlife are to be treated with utmost respect in the parks. Keep your distance—at least 100 yards if possible—from any wild animal.

WATERBORNE ILLNESSES Two waterborne hazards are *Giardia* and *Campylobacter,* with symptoms that wreak havoc on the human digestive system. Untreated water from the parks' lakes and streams should be boiled for at least 5 minutes before consumption, treated with iodine pills, or pumped through a fine-mesh water filter specifically designed to remove bacteria.

WHAT TO DO IF YOU GET SICK AWAY FROM HOME

In Yosemite National Park, the **Yosemite Medical Clinic** (✆ **209/ 372-4637**), in Yosemite Village, is open daily in summer and Monday through Friday the rest of the year. In Sequoia & Kings Canyon, the closest medical facilities are in the gateway towns of Fresno, Visalia, and Three Rivers.

6 SAFETY

Following are some general safety tips for visitors to Yosemite and Sequoia & Kings Canyon:

- Although some of the bridges that cross rivers and streams look inviting, resist the temptation to use them as diving boards—it's not only dangerous, but also illegal.
- Trails, especially ones over rock and granite, can be slick. Be especially careful along any rivers or creeks, such as Mist Trail in Yosemite, where wind and water can make for treacherous conditions.

- Always carry more than enough water, especially when going into higher elevations where our bodies require more hydration.
- Under no circumstances should food be left in tents, cabins, or cars. There are storage lockers and bear-proof containers throughout the park—use them.
- Under no circumstances should you feed a bear—or any wild animal, for that matter.
- Always carry a map if you go hiking, even for short day hikes.

CLOTHING & EQUIPMENT

Nothing will ruin a trip to the parks faster than sore or wet feet. Take some time planning your travel wardrobe. Bring comfortable walking shoes that are broken in, even if you plan to keep walking to a minimum. If you want to do some serious hiking, get sturdy boots that support your ankles and wick away water. Early in the season, trails may be wet or muddy; late in the fall, you can get snowed on. The more popular trails are sometimes also used by horses, which can make stream crossings a mucky mess.

Wear clothing in layers, and bring a small backpack or fanny pack so that you can take those layers off and on as the temperature, altitude, and your physical exertion change. Cotton is a no-no in the backcountry; synthetic fabrics are recommended because they dry much faster. Gloves or mittens are useful before the park heats up, or in the evening when it cools down again, *even in summer.*

The atmosphere is thin at higher altitudes, so protect your skin. Bring a strong sunblock, a hat with a brim, and sunglasses. Insect repellent, water bottles, and a first-aid kit are also recommended.

7 SPECIALIZED TRAVEL RESOURCES

In addition to the destination-specific resources listed below, please visit Frommers.com for additional specialized travel resources.

GAY & LESBIAN TRAVELERS

Yosemite and Sequoia & Kings Canyon are generally gay-friendly. However, gay culture and nightlife are very limited in the gateway towns.

TRAVELERS WITH DISABILITIES

People visit these parks to witness their beauty, and that can be done in a host of different ways—you don't have to hike 5 miles or climb to the top of a waterfall. Some of the most rewarding moments come from quiet, still observation.

Be sure to inquire about the National Park Service's free **Interagency Access Pass,** available to the blind and those with permanent disabilities.

In Yosemite, there are some fairly level paved trails around the valley floor, including the ones to Mirror Lake and Happy Isles, and the paved bike trail is also accessible to wheelchairs (see "Bicycling," in chapter 4). Ask for information on accessible points when making reservations. An accessibility brochure is available at park entrances and visitor centers, and wheelchairs can be rented at the **Yosemite Medical Clinic** (℃ **209/372-4637**) and the **Yosemite Lodge Bike Rental Stand** (℃ **209/372-1208**). In Sequoia & Kings Canyon, the visitor centers in the Foothills, Lodgepole, and Grant Grove are wheelchair accessible. Paved trails lead to the General Sherman Tree and General Grant Tree. In Giant Forest, there are a few paved trails (including Big Trees Trail). There are modified picnic tables at Hospital Rock and Big Stump. Special requests should be directed to ℃ **559/565-3134.**

Wheelchair Getaways (℃ **800/642-2042** or 859/873-4973; www.wheelchair-getaways.com) rents specialized vans with wheelchair lifts and other features for those with disabilities, with outlets in most Western states.

FAMILY TRAVEL

Yosemite schedules a number of children's programs. Kids ages 3 to 6 can join the Little Cubs, and those from 7 to 13 can become Junior Rangers, by completing projects in a booklet ($3 for Little Cubs and $3.50 for Junior Rangers); those in the Junior Ranger program also collect a bag of trash and participate in a ranger program. Upon completion, Little Cubs receive a button; Junior Rangers get a patch. The booklets are available at the Nature Center at Happy Isles, Yosemite Valley and Tuolumne Meadows visitor centers, and the Wawona and Big Oak Flat information stations.

Free ranger-led walks and talks, many suitable for kids, are held at various locations throughout the park. The programs vary by season, so check your *Yosemite Guide* (handed out at park entrances) to find out what's happening during your visit. The Happy Isles Nature Center (shuttle-bus stop no. 16) has displays and dioramas of park animals that children will enjoy.

During the summer, Sequoia & Kings Canyon offer ranger-led walks aimed at families, as well as a campfire program at Lodgepole (check at visitor centers for the current schedule). In addition, the parks have a Junior Ranger program in which children get booklets and complete various activities to become Junior Rangers. Another child-friendly option is the Beetle Rock Education Center near the Giant Forest Museum, open on summer weekends only.

SENIOR TRAVEL

Anyone 62 or older can get an **Interagency Senior Pass** for a one-time fee of $10. The passes are available at any entrance point to Yosemite or Sequoia & Kings Canyon. The Interagency Senior Pass must be purchased in person in order to verify age.

TRAVELERS WITH PETS

Pets are not particularly welcome at national parks. In Yosemite, pets are not allowed on unpaved trails or in buildings; they must be leashed at all times and may never be left alone. Pets are permitted in all campgrounds except Camp 4 Walk-In, Tamarack Flat, and Porcupine Flat. There's a **dog kennel** (© **209/372-8348**), open daily from 8am to 4:30pm in the summer, at the stable in Yosemite Valley. Dogs must be at least 6 months old and weigh over 20 pounds (or under 20 lb. in a dog carrier); a license and proof of current shots must be faxed over beforehand. The fee is $9.50 per day; call for reservations.

Similar regulations apply at Sequoia & Kings Canyon. Pets are allowed in all campgrounds but not on any trails or in the backcountry. A good rule of thumb issued by the National Park Service: You can take your pet wherever you can take your car, but keep it on a leash.

---

8 SUSTAINABLE TOURISM

These parks are incredibly beautiful and a joy to experience, and it is our responsibility as park visitors to keep them that way. Don't feed the animals. Don't litter. Don't take anything home that you didn't buy or bring with you. Share trails and walkways, and stay on them. If this sounds like something you learned in grade school, it is, but sometimes people need a gentle reminder that 50 million years of work deserves respect.

It's relatively easy to be a good outdoor citizen—it's mostly common sense. Pack out all trash, stay on established trails, be careful not to pollute water, and do your best to have as little impact on the environment as possible. Some hikers go further, carrying a small trash bag to pick up litter. As the park service likes to remind us, protecting our national parks is everyone's responsibility.

Nonetheless, heavy summer auto traffic and the annual impact of millions of human beings have raised questions about the sustainability of these national parks. But a visit to Yosemite and Sequoia & Kings Canyon can still be a relatively green vacation. In Yosemite, concessionaire **DNC Parks & Resorts at Yosemite** (© 801/559-4884; www.yosemitepark.com) has implemented numerous environmental initiatives, including a recycling program, nonnative plant–removal initiatives, and biodiesel-powered vehicles. Campgrounds have recycling bins near the entrances.

Perhaps the best way to think about sustainability is by connecting with the parks' wild soul via hikes on the trails and overnights in the campgrounds. One of the best ways to lessen one's impact is to go off the grid on an overnight backpacking trip. Backpacking is a refreshing counterpoint to modern life that will give perspective on the issues of sustainability and personal energy dependence. For more on backpacking, see "Special Permits & Passes," below, and sections on each park's backcountry in chapters 4 and 7. Also see **Leave No Trace** (www.lnt.org) for more on the backpacker's ethic to leave any campsite in the same condition—or better—than when you found it.

9 SPECIAL-INTEREST TRIPS & ESCORTED GENERAL-INTEREST TOURS

ACADEMIC TRIPS

The nonprofit **Yosemite Association** (© 209/379-2321 or 379-2646; www.yosemite.org) offers dozens of **Outdoor Adventures ★**, covering subjects from backpacking to natural history to photography. Most of the programs are multiday, with charges of about $100 per person per day (not including lodging and meals), and often include hikes or backpacking trips.

Sequoia Field Institute ★, in Three Rivers (© 559/565-4251; www.sequoiahistory.org/sfi/sfi.htm), offers a number of field seminars in and around Sequoia & Kings Canyon. The programs typically run from 1 to 4 days, with fees ranging from around $50 for the 1-day seminars to $100 and up for the multiday programs. Topics vary, but are likely to include subjects such as mountain wildflowers, black bears, photography, and, of course, giant sequoias. Some seminars have minimum age requirements, and some are physically demanding.

ADVENTURE TRIPS

Part of concessionaire DNC Parks & Resorts at Yosemite, **Yosemite Mountaineering** (📞 **209/372-8344;** www.yosemitemountaineering.com) offers a variety of guided climbing and backpacking trips.

Southern Yosemite Mountain Guides, based in Santa Cruz (📞 **800/231-4575;** www.symg.com), offers hiking, backpacking, fishing, and rock-climbing trips. Trips last from a day to over a week; prices run about $150 to $200 a day.

California Alpine Guides, based in Mammoth Lakes (📞 **877/686-2546;** www.californiaalpineguides.com), offers multiday climbing and backpacking trips in Yosemite and Sequoia for about $150 to $200 a day.

Austin-Lehman Adventures, based in Billings, Mont. (📞 **800/575-1540** or 406/655-4591; www.austinlehman.com), offers guided family-oriented multiday hiking tours in Yosemite. Five-night trips run about $2,000 per person, lodging included.

Backroads, based in Berkeley (📞 **800/462-2848** or 510/527-1555; www.backroads.com), offers a variety of guided biking and hiking tours in the Yosemite area. Rates are about $2,000 to $3,000 per person for 6 days.

The **World Outdoors,** based in Boulder, Colorado (📞 **800/488-8483** or 303/413-0938; www.theworldoutdoors.com), offers a variety of trips, including multi-sport adventures that include hiking and biking in Yosemite. Rates range from $1,900 to $2,600 per person for 6 days.

Additionally, both the **Yosemite Bug** and **Evergreen Lodge** have excellent in-house recreation programs that include guided trips in and around the park. See "Lodging" in chapter 5.

10 STAYING CONNECTED

When it comes to modern telecommunications, Yosemite and Sequoia & Kings Canyon national parks have limited infrastructure: Lack of connectivity is the rule, not the exception. These are not the best destinations for those who need to check e-mail every minute—or even every day. Many of the lodgings in the parks lack Internet connections, and even in-room telephones are not the norm, but cell service is fairly good and continues to expand.

CELLPHONES The parks have several cell towers in developed areas. Cell service is widely available on the floor of Yosemite Valley; in Sequoia & Kings Canyon, it is available in the villages but largely unavailable on the roads and in wilderness areas. Cell service is available in all of the gateway cities.

INTERNET & E-MAIL   In Yosemite, Internet access is available at Degnan's Cafe on fee-based terminals. Wi-Fi is available at Yosemite Lodge for a fee. In Sequoia & Kings Canyon, Wi-Fi is available at Wuksachi Lodge and in Grant Grove Village. Internet access is widely available in all of the gateways.

11 TIPS ON ACCOMMODATIONS

In the parks, your options are fairly limited; the finite number of rooms and seemingly limitless number of peak-season visitors make for high occupancy and rates. And the fact that many of the parks' hostelries have historic designations might mean they don't fit some visitors' modern tastes.

For information on much of the lodging within Yosemite National Park, contact **DNC Parks & Resorts at Yosemite,** P.O. Box 578, Yosemite National Park, CA 95389 (© **801/559-5000;** www.yosemitepark.com). For lodging information and reservations at Wuksachi Lodge in the Giant Forest area of Sequoia National Park, call © **866/807-3598** or 801/559-4930, or visit www.visitsequoia.com. For information on Grant Grove, John Muir, or Cedar Grove lodges in Kings Canyon National Park, call © **866/522-6966** or 559/335-5500, or visit www.sequoia-kingscanyon.com.

In the gateway cities, there is more variety, from dorm-style hostels to luxury ski resorts. House-swapping is a possibility in many of the gateway cities, especially Visalia and Oakhurst.

12 SPECIAL PERMITS & PASSES

American parks and monuments are some of the biggest travel bargains in the world. If you plan to visit a number of national parks and monuments within a year, buy an **America the Beautiful—National Parks and Federal Interagency Annual Pass** for $80 (good for 365 days from the date of purchase at nearly all federal preserves). Anyone age 62 or older can get an **Interagency Senior Pass** for a one-time fee of $10, and people who are blind or who have permanent disabilities can obtain an **Interagency Access Pass,** which costs nothing. All passes are available at any park entrance point or visitor center. While the Interagency Senior and Interagency Access passes must be purchased in person (to verify age or disability), Interagency Annual Passes are also available online at **http://store.usgs.gov/pass**.

You'll need a **backcountry permit** to camp overnight in the wilderness sections of these parks. (For details, see chapter 3, "Exploring Yosemite," chapter 4, "Hikes & Other Outdoor Pursuits in Yosemite," chapter 6, "Exploring Sequoia & Kings Canyon," and chapter 7, "Hikes & Other Outdoor Pursuits in Sequoia & Kings Canyon.") Reserving a permit costs $5, plus $5 per person in Yosemite and $15 per group in Sequoia & Kings Canyon; it's a good idea to reserve one in advance during the high season. For permits in Yosemite, call ℂ **209/372-0740** or stop by any Wilderness Permit Station. In Sequoia & Kings Canyon, call ℂ **559/565-3766.** Information is also available online at **www.nps.gov/yose** for Yosemite or **www.nps.gov/seki** for Sequoia & Kings Canyon.

Elsewhere in the parks, the usual permits and regulations apply. All anglers 16 and over must have valid California fishing licenses.

13 PLANNING A BACKCOUNTRY TRIP

While you can find the particulars for Yosemite and Sequoia & Kings Canyon in their respective chapters (see chapters 3 and 6), the following are some general things for you to keep in mind when planning a backcountry trip.

REGULATIONS

The theme in the backcountry is "leave no trace," and that means packing out any garbage you take in, not bringing pets, and staying on designated trails and reusing existing designated campsites so you don't leave scars on the landscape. Fires are allowed only in established fire rings, and only dead and downed material may be used for firewood; fires are prohibited in some areas, but backpacking stoves are allowed throughout the parks. You must have a park permit for overnight stays in the backcountry. For more information on "leave no trace" ethics, see **www.lnt.org**.

PERSONAL SAFETY ISSUES

It's best not to backpack alone, but if you must, be sure that you have told both park rangers and friends where you'll be and how long you'll be gone. Don't leave the parking lot without the following gear: a compass, topographical maps, a first-aid kit, bug repellent, toilet paper and a trowel of some sort, a flashlight, matches, a knife, a rope for hanging food supplies in a tree, and a bell or other noisemaker that hopefully will alert any bears in the neighborhood to your presence, as well as a tent, a stove, and a sleeping bag. At this altitude, sunscreen and sunglasses with UV protection are a wise addition. A recently developed bear repellent generically referred to as "pepper spray," available in most sporting-goods stores, has proven successful in countering bear attacks. You'll also need iodine pills or a good water filter because that seemingly clear stream is filled with parasites that are likely to cause intestinal disorders. If you don't have iodine or a filter, boil water for at least 5 minutes before you drink it.

Exploring Yosemite

Yosemite's towering geologic formations, lush mead-
ows, tumbling rivers, and spectacular waterfalls attract travelers from
around the world. Yosemite is home to 3 of the world's 10 tallest
waterfalls and the largest single piece of exposed granite on the planet.
It boasts some of the world's largest trees and what is possibly the
most recognized rock formation. And you don't have to be a moun-
taineer to enjoy the beauty of the park—Yosemite's most popular
attractions are accessible to everyone, whether you want to hike
around or just stand and stare. No matter where you go, you'll find a
view worth remembering.

1 ESSENTIALS

ACCESS/ENTRY POINTS

There are four entrances to Yosemite: the Big Oak Flat Entrance and
the Arch Rock Entrance from the west, the South Entrance, and the
Tioga Pass Entrance from the east. See the "Yosemite National Park"
map (p. 2) to orient yourself. Upon arrival, make sure to get a copy
of the biweekly *Yosemite Guide* for up-to-date information on ranger
programs and other park events and activities.

VISITOR CENTERS & INFORMATION

In the park, the biggest visitor center is the **Valley Visitor Center,** in
Yosemite Village (© **209/372-0200**), which provides all sorts of
information, offers daily ranger programs, and is conveniently located
near restaurants and shopping. You can talk with park rangers about
your plans for exploring the park, check out bulletin boards that
display information on current road conditions and campsite availability (they also serve as a message board for visitors), and view several exhibits on the park, its geologic history, and the history of the
valley. This center provides information on bears and also explores the
impact that humans have on the park. A shop sells maps, books,
videos, postcards, posters, and the like.

Nearby is the **Yosemite Valley Wilderness Center,** with high-country
maps; information on necessary hiking and camping equipment; trail

information; and a ranger on hand to answer questions, issue permits, and offer advice about the high country.

Information is also available at the **Wawona Information Station** and the **Big Oak Flat Information Station.** In the high country, stop in at the **Tuolumne Meadows Visitor Center** (*©* **209/372-0263,** although it's always best to call 209/372-0200 in summer). For questions about visitor-related services, including tours and accommodations, call *©* **209/372-1000.**

FEES

It costs $20 per car per week to enter the valley, or $10 per person per week if arriving on bicycle, on motorcycle, or on foot. The Yosemite Pass, for $40, covers entry into the park for a year. Also see "Special Permits & Passes," in chapter 2.

Camping at a Yosemite campground costs $5 to $20 a night (*©* **877/444-6777;** www.recreation.gov). It's best to book as far in advance as possible if you are planning to camp during the summer, especially in Yosemite Valley. If you're unable to get your desired dates, it's worth checking back—cancellations do occur. Reservations are accepted up to 5 months in advance, beginning on the 15th of each month. For example, a camper wanting a reservation for August 1 can apply no earlier than February 15. Additional campground information is available by phone or online (*©* **209/372-0200;** www.nps.gov/yose/planyourvisit/camping.htm).

REGULATIONS

The regulations here are similar to those at most other national parks—don't damage the resources, keep pets and bikes off the trails, observe campground quiet hours, and so on—but this is also **bear country,** so the storage of food, or anything that bears might think of as food, is also strictly regulated. In many cases, you'll need to place food and items that smell like they might be food (perfume and even toothpaste) in bear-proof canisters or lockers. Regulations are posted throughout the park, and you'll also receive information when you enter the park, but we strongly suggest that you carry as little food, cosmetics, and toiletries as possible.

2 ORIENTATION

All four main entrances to the park meet in Yosemite Valley, the most popular of the park's three destination points (the other two being Tuolumne Meadows and Wawona). The valley is a mile wide and 7 miles long, set at about 4,000 feet above sea level. The granite walls of Half Dome, El Capitan, and Glacier Point tower another 4,000 feet overhead. The picturesque Merced River, fed by several small brooks and creeks, winds lazily through the length of Yosemite Valley.

It's relatively easy to find your way around Yosemite. All road signs are clear and visible. At first, Yosemite Valley might seem to be a confusing series of roadways, but you'll soon realize that all roads lead to a one-way loop that hugs the valley's perimeter. It is easy to find yourself heading in the wrong direction, so be alert whenever you merge and just follow the signs.

We recommend visitors use year-round shuttle-bus service in the Yosemite Valley; Wawona and Tuolumne Meadows offer a similar service during the summer months only. Driving in any of these places during peak season—or even off season in the valley—is not fun, so use the shuttles as much as possible.

YOSEMITE VALLEY

Most people come to Yosemite to see this giant study in shadow and light. In spring, after the winter snow begins melting in the high country, waterfalls encircle Yosemite Valley, shimmering like a diamond necklace. There are wide, beautiful meadows, towering trees, and the ever-present sound of rushing water in the background. The great irony is that the original park boundaries, established in 1890, excluded the valley. In addition to the natural phenomena found throughout the valley, there are a number of historical attractions worth exploring as well.

Yosemite Valley contains three developed areas: **Yosemite Village, Yosemite Lodge at the Falls,** and **Curry Village.** Except for the Ahwahnee Hotel—which is about midway between Yosemite and Curry villages—all the hotels, restaurants, and shops can be found in these areas. Curry Village (also called Camp Curry) and Yosemite Lodge offer the bulk of the park's overnight accommodations. Curry Village is near shuttle-bus stop nos. 13A, 13B, 14, 15, 20, and 21. Yosemite Lodge is served by stop no. 8. Both locations have restaurants and a small grocery. The lodge has a large public swimming pool, and Curry Village has an ice rink open in winter.

Yosemite Village is the largest developed region within the valley and is served by shuttle-bus stop nos. 1, 2, 4, 5, 9, and 10. It is home to the park's largest visitor center and the headquarters for the National Park Service in Yosemite. The village also has a host of shops and services, including a grocery store, restaurants, the valley's only medical clinic, a dentist, a post office, and an ATM.

Check out the **Yosemite Pioneer Cemetery,** a peaceful graveyard in the shade of tall sequoias, with headstones dating back to the 1800s. There are about 36 marked graves, identifiable by horizontal slabs of rock, some etched with crude or faded writing. There are some Yosemite history notables buried here, such as James Lamon, an early settler who was known for his apple trees—they still bear fruit—and who died in 1875. Pick up the self-guiding booklet at the visitor center.

Next door, you'll find the **Yosemite Museum** and the **Indian Cultural Exhibit.** Both attractions are free and provide a historic picture of the park, before and after it was settled and secured as a national treasure. The museum entrance is marked by a crowd-pleaser: the cross section of a 1,000-year-old sequoia with memorable dates identified on the tree's rings. The tree section was cut in 1919 from a tree that fell in the Mariposa Grove south of the valley in Wawona. The Indian Cultural Exhibit strives to explain the life of the American Indians who once lived here, and members of regional tribes regularly speak or give demonstrations of traditional arts such as basket weaving. The Yosemite Museum Shop is next door and sells books and traditional Indian arts and crafts.

The village of the **Ahwahneeche** (a reproduction of a real Ahwahneeche village) is behind the museum and the Indian Cultural Exhibit. The village offers a free self-guided walking tour accessible from the back door of the visitor center. This exhibit guides visitors through the transformations of the Ahwahneeche, the tribe that inhabited Yosemite Valley until the mid-1850s. The village includes a ceremonial roundhouse that's still in use.

The **Ansel Adams Gallery** (© **888/361-7622** or 209/372-4413; www.anseladams.com) sells prints and cards of images made by this famed photographer. The shop also serves as a small gallery for current artisans, with some of their works for sale.

Just a mile east of Yosemite Village on a narrow, dead-end road is the majestic old **Ahwahnee Hotel** (see chapter 5, "Where to Stay & Eat in Yosemite"). Take the shuttle bus to stop no. 3. It's definitely worth a visit for anyone interested in architecture and design.

The **Yosemite Valley Chapel** is located on the south side of the Merced River, shuttle-bus stop no. 11. From the bus stop, walk across the bridge and to the left for just under a quarter-mile. Schedules for the worship services held in the chapel are posted in the *Yosemite Guide* newspaper and are available by phone (© **209/372-4831**).

The **LeConte Memorial Lodge** is an educational center and library at shuttle-bus stop no. 12. Built in 1903, in honor of a Uni-

To Upper Yosemite Fall

Lower Yosemite Fall

Lost and Found

Yosemite Museum and Indian Cultural Exhibit

Yosemite Village *4000 ft.*

U.S. Court
Valley Visitor Center

Columbia Rock

Parking

Yosemite Lodge at the Falls

Yosemite Creek

Park Headquarters

Medical Clinic

Village Store

The Ahwahnee

Parking

Sunnyside (walk-in)

Yosemite Valley Chapel

Housekeeping Camp

Le Conte Memorial Lodge

Northside Dr. (one way)

Merced River

Union Point

Moran Point

Staircase Falls

Southside Dr. (one way)

Glacier Point 7214 ft.

Parking (summer only)

← To all other points in park and park exits

Sentinel Rock 7038 ft.

Sentinel Creek

Sentinel Fall

To Taft Point

SENTINEL DOME 8122 ft.

Glacier Point Rd. (closed Nov. - May)

versity of California geologist named Joseph LeConte, the Tudor-style granite building hosts a number of free educational programs and talks, which are listed in the *Yosemite Guide.*

Beyond Curry Village at the valley's far eastern end is the **Happy Isles Nature Center,** shuttle-bus stop no. 16. Summer hours are from 9am to 5pm daily; it is closed spring, fall, and winter. The nature center offers exhibits and books about the varied animal and plant life found in Yosemite; it's a super place for children to explore. The park's Little Cub and Junior Ranger programs, described under "Family Travel" in the "Specialized Travel Resources" section of chapter 2, are held here as well. Happy Isles is named for three nearby inlets labeled by Yosemite's guardian in 1880.

NORTH OF THE VALLEY

Hetch Hetchy and **Tuolumne Meadows** are remarkably different regions located on opposite sides of the park. Hetch Hetchy is on the

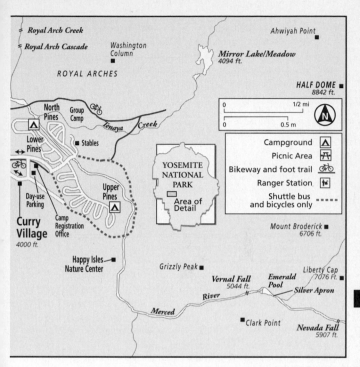

park's western border and can be reached by taking the Evergreen Road turnoff just outside the park's Big Oak Flat Entrance. Tuolumne Meadows is on the park's eastern border, just inside Tioga Pass, and is inaccessible by motor vehicle during the winter. (Tioga Rd. is the road that leads to the meadows.)

Impressions

The big Tuolumne Meadows are flowery lawns, lying along the South Fork of the Tuolumne River . . . here the mountains seem to have been cleared away or sit back, so that wide-open views may be had in every direction.

—John Muir

> ## ⓜ Moments **Alpenglow**
>
> You're in for a real treat if you position yourself with a view of the mountains and granite outcroppings around sunrise or sunset. The light of the rising and setting sun casts a rich, brilliant pink glow (known as alpenglow) on the landscape. This is a terrific time for photographing the area.

Hetch Hetchy is home to the park's reservoir, passionately opposed by the famed conservationist John Muir and reviled by environmentalists to this day. Many believe that losing the battle over the reservoir exhausted Muir and hastened his death. Muir passed away in 1914, a year after the bill was signed to fund the dam project. Construction on the dam began in 1919 and was completed in 1923. The reservoir provides San Francisco with drinking water; the dam generates a bit of electricity for the city as well.

South of Hetch Hetchy are two large stands of giant sequoias. The Merced and Tuolumne groves offer a quiet alternative to the Mariposa Grove of Big Trees in Wawona. Both groves are accessible only on foot. The Merced Grove is a 4-mile round-trip walk that begins about 4½ miles inside the Big Oak Flat Entrance. Although the trees here don't mirror the majesty of the Mariposa Grove, the solitude makes this a real treat for hikers. The Tuolumne Grove (about 25 trees) can be reached by a 1-mile hike (2 hr. round-trip).

To get into Yosemite's **high country,** go about 1½ hours east along Tioga Road, which is closed in winter between Big Oak Flat and Tioga Pass. (You'll need skis or snowshoes to access this area during the winter.) This subalpine region is low on amenities, making it the frequent haunt of those who enjoy roughing it, but even cushy-soft couch potatoes can enjoy the beauty up here. Glistening granite domes tower above lush green meadows, which are cut by silver swaths of streams and lakes. Many of Yosemite's longer hikes begin or pass through here. The high country is explored at length in chapter 4, "Hikes & Other Outdoor Pursuits in Yosemite." There are some worthwhile sights here for anyone willing to venture away from the valley masses.

Olmsted Point ★★, located midway between White Wolf and Tuolumne Meadows, offers one of the most spectacular vistas anywhere in the park. Here the enormous walls of the Tenaya Canyon are exposed, and an endless view stretches all the way to Yosemite Valley.

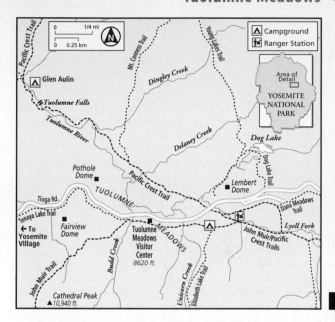

In the distance are Cloud's Rest and the rear of Half Dome. To the east, Tenaya Lake, one of the park's larger lakes (and an easily accessible one), glistens like a sapphire.

About 8 miles east of Tenaya Lake is **Tuolumne Meadows,** a huge subalpine area surrounded by domes and steep granite formations that offer exhilarating climbs. The meadow is a beautiful place to hike and fish, or just to admire the scenery while escaping the crowds of Yosemite Valley. Facing to the north of the meadow is Lembert Dome, at about two o'clock; and then working clockwise, Johnson Peak, at seven o'clock; Unicorn Peak, at eight o'clock; Fairview Dome, at ten o'clock; and Pothole Dome, at eleven o'clock. Up the road is the central region of Tuolumne, where you'll find a visitor center, a campground, canvas tent-cabins, and a store. Continue east to reach Tioga Lake and Tioga Pass.

SOUTH OF THE VALLEY

This region, which includes Wawona and the Mariposa Grove of Big Trees, is densely forested. A handful of granite rock formations dot the area, but they are nothing like those found elsewhere. En route to Wawona from the valley, you'll come across several wonderful views of Yosemite Valley. **Tunnel View,** a turnout accessed just before passing through a long tunnel along Wawona Road, provides one of the park's most recognizable vistas, memorialized on film by photographer Ansel Adams. To the right is Bridalveil Fall, opposite El Capitan. Half Dome lies straight ahead.

Halfway between Yosemite Valley and Wawona is Glacier Point Road (closed in winter past the turnoff to Badger Pass Ski Area), which runs 16 miles to spectacular **Glacier Point ★★★**. From the parking area, it's a short hike to an amazing overlook that provides a view of the glacier-carved granite rock formations all along the valley and beyond. At this point you will be at eye level with Half Dome, which looks close enough to reach out and touch. Far below, Yosemite Valley resembles a green-carpeted ant farm. There are also some pretty sights of obscure waterfalls that are not visible from the valley floor. Glacier Point has a geology hut and a day lodge for wintertime cross-country skiers. The day lodge morphs into a gift store/snack shack during the rest of the year. Glacier Point and the lodge are accessible both on foot and by bus (see "Organized Tours & Ranger Programs," later in this chapter).

Continue south on Wawona Road to reach **Wawona,** a small town that runs deep with history, located 30 miles from the valley. It was settled in 1856 by homesteader Galen Clark, who built a rustic way station for travelers en route from Mariposa to Yosemite. The property's next owners, the Washburn brothers, built much of what is today the Wawona Hotel, including the large white building to the right of the main hotel, which was constructed in 1876. The two-story hotel annex went up 3 years later. When Congress established Yosemite National Park in 1890 and charged the U.S. Army with managing it, Wawona was chosen as the Army's headquarters. For 16 summers, the cavalry out of San Francisco occupied the camp and mapped the park. When Yosemite Valley was added to the park after the turn of the 20th century, the cavalry picked up and relocated to the valley.

Near the Wawona Hotel are Hill's Studio and the Pioneer Yosemite History Center. The studio keeps sporadic hours that are hard to pin down but are listed in the *Yosemite Guide;* this is the former workspace of noted 19th-century painter Thomas Hill. Hill painted a number of award-winning landscapes, including some recognizable ones of Yosemite.

The Pioneer Center offers a self-guided walking tour of cabins and buildings that were moved to this site in 1961 from various locations in the park. Each building represents a different period in Yosemite's short history. During the summer, National Park Service interpreters dress in period clothing and act out characters from the park's past. To reach the center, walk across the covered bridge. An entertaining 10-minute stagecoach ride is offered during the summer for a small fee.

Nearby, the **Mariposa Grove** is a stand of giant sequoias, some of which have been around for 3,000 years. They stretch almost 300 feet tall, are 50 feet in circumference, and weigh an average of 2 million pounds. The 500 trees here are divided into the Upper Grove and the Lower Grove. The easiest way to see the trees is from the open-air **tram** (© **209/372-4386** for reservations) that runs May through October. Cost is $26 for adults, $24 for seniors, and $18 for children; kids 4 and under ride free. Trams leave from the Mariposa Grove parking area; call for current hours. A guide provides commentary during the trip, which lasts about an hour and 15 minutes. The tram makes regular stops at the Grizzly Giant, Wawona Tunnel Tree, and Mariposa Grove Museum. It's worth hopping out and walking around as often as possible. Just take the next tram back. All of the area is also accessible on foot. It is an uphill walk to the upper grove, 2.5 miles each way.

The Grizzly Giant is the largest tree in the grove. At "just" 200 feet, it is shorter than some of its neighbors, but its trunk measures more than 30 feet in diameter at the base. A huge limb halfway up the tree measures 6 feet in diameter and is bigger than many of the "young" trees in the grove.

The Wawona Tunnel Tree had a tunnel 10 feet high and 26 feet long cut through it in 1881. Thousands of visitors were photographed driving through the tree before it toppled during a snowstorm in 1969, its death finally caused by heavy snow. No one saw the tree fall. Another tunnel tree, the California Tree, had a tunnel cut in 1895 and still stands near the Grizzly Giant, beckoning visitors to walk through it.

The Mariposa Grove Museum resides in Galen Clark's first building. It was last refurbished in 1981 and is usually open from late spring into the fall, featuring various exhibits. Books and educational materials are also sold here from late spring into fall.

3 THE HIGHLIGHTS

Spectacular **Yosemite Falls** ★★★ is a three-part waterfall that stretches 2,425 feet skyward, making it one of the tallest waterfalls in the world. In spring, snow runoff makes it a magnificent spectacle as spray crashes to the base of the falls, leaving visitors drenched. In the winter, cold temperatures help form a cone at the base of the waterfall, sometimes reaching 200 feet high—it looks like a giant upside-down snow cone. You can reach the base of Yosemite Falls by taking the shuttle bus to stop no. 6. It is also an easy walk from any parking lot near Yosemite Lodge.

Picturesque **Mirror Lake** ★, named for its nearly perfect reflection of the surrounding scenery, is slowly filling with sediments, and depending on the spring runoff, may be little more than a watering hole by late summer. Still, the lake captures beautiful images of Half Dome and North Dome, which tower above. It is surrounded by forest and has a fairly level, paved trail along its banks, which also offer places to sunbathe and picnic. It's accessible (by vehicle) to people with disabilities; there's a 60-foot elevation gain. Take the shuttle to stop no. 17. The **Mist Trail to Vernal Fall** shows the power behind the water that flows through Yosemite. The trail itself can be slick and treacherous, but it is a pretty walk up 500 steps to the top of the

Map legend and labels:
- Wawona Point
- Summer Hiking Trail to Wawona
- UPPER GROVE
- Fallen Wawona Tunnel Tree 6600 ft.
- Mariposa Grove Museum 6400 ft.
- Outer Loop Trail
- YOSEMITE NATIONAL PARK
- Area of Detail
- LOWER GROVE
- Picnic Area
- Ranger Station
- Restrooms
- Tram Route − − −
- Grizzly Giant 6000 ft.
- Parking
- Free Shuttle Bus Stop (seasonal)
- Tram Boarding Area 5600 ft.
- Gift Shop
- Free Shuttle Bus Stop (seasonal)
- Mariposa Grove Rd
- To Wawona South Entrance
- 0   1/2 mi
- 0   0.5 km

EXPLORING YOSEMITE

3

THE HIGHLIGHTS

waterfall (see chapter 4). Miniature rainbows dot the trail as mist from the waterfall splashes below and ricochets back onto the trail. This walk is sometimes closed in winter due to ice, but there is a winter route to the top of the fall. (For the winter route, see the hike descriptions in chapter 4.)

The remnants of a recent rockslide can be seen behind the **Happy Isles Nature Center.** Several years ago, a granite slab collapsed with such force that it blew over hundreds of trees, claimed one life, and filled the valley with dust. Park officials decided to leave the landscape pretty much as it was post-slide, as a reminder of the tremendous geologic forces that shaped (and are still shaping) the park.

The **view from Glacier Point ★★★** is one of the most spectacular vistas in the park. From this point, far above the valley floor, visitors will find themselves at eye level with Half Dome and hundreds of feet above most of the park's waterfalls. The white and silver rocks offer a stark contrast against the sky. To reach Glacier Point in summer, take one of the buses (check at tour desks for information) or drive south of the valley on Wawona Road to the turnoff for Glacier

Point Road. Follow the winding road to the parking lot (allow about 45 min. from the valley) and walk a few hundred yards to the lookout. In winter, the road is closed and Glacier Point is accessible only on skis or snowshoes.

A **drive toward the high country** on Tioga Road offers other breathtaking views. To our thinking, some of the grandest sights are at **Olmsted Point ★★**, which provides a panoramic view of the granite landscape. There are nearby picnic spots at picturesque Tenaya Lake. A bit farther is the emerald-green Tuolumne Meadows, dotted with thousands of wildflowers during late spring and summer (see "Exploring the Backcountry" in chapter 4).

An **off-season visit** to Yosemite Valley, especially in winter, offers unique beauty plus the peace and quiet that was once commonplace. And although the high country is inaccessible by car—Tioga Pass Road and Glacier Point Road are usually closed to vehicles from mid-fall to early June, depending on snowfall—the valley becomes more accessible, as the number of visitors is greatly reduced. Snow dusts the granite peaks and valley floor, bends trees, and creates a winter wonderland for visitors. Lodging rates drop, and it is slightly easier to secure accommodations or a campground site, but even a day trip can be rewarding. Although many animals hibernate during the cold months, this is the best time of year to see the valley as it was before it became such a popular place.

4 HOW TO SEE THE PARK IN 1 OR 2 DAYS

This is a park that begs for an extended visit, but those with a limited amount of time will also have an enjoyable experience, especially if they make use of the park's shuttle bus. The bus is free, easy to use, and operates year-round (though with fewer stops in winter). For that reason, we've included shuttle-bus stop numbers wherever possible throughout the valley sections in this book. Bus stops are well marked and within easy walking distance of all parking lots.

You can get on and off the shuttles at any point, but be sure to stop in the **Valley Visitor Center** (shuttle-bus stop nos. 5 and 9) for an orientation on the forces that carved the valley.

If you're not interested in taking off and exploring alone, opt for one of the guided tours (see "Organized Tours & Ranger Programs," below).

The base of **Lower Yosemite Fall** (shuttle-bus stop no. 6) is an easy walk from either Yosemite Village or Yosemite Lodge. From the base, you can see a portion of the magnificent water show. During peak runoff, it's not uncommon to get wet, as the force of the fall sends spray in every direction. In late winter and early spring, a huge snow cone caused by freezing water rises up to 200 feet from the base of this fall. The hike up the fall is described in detail in chapter 4.

Happy Isles (shuttle-bus stop no. 16) is another major attraction. Located at the convergence of several inlets, the valley's nature center is an especially great stop for those traveling with kids, but the area gets most of its traffic because it is also the trail head for Vernal and Nevada falls, two picturesque staircase waterfalls that can only be reached by foot. Both hikes are described in chapter 4.

Next, we recommend a visit to **Mirror Lake** (shuttle-bus stop no. 17), a small lake named for the near-perfect way it reflects the surrounding scenery. It's slowly filling up with silt and is less dramatic and mirrorlike than it used to be, but its shore still offers a beautiful view of Half Dome. This short stroll is well marked and described in chapter 4.

If you still have more time to explore, choose anything that piques your interest from a variety of hikes and activities. To make the most of your time, stick with the recommendations we list throughout the following chapters.

5 SEEING THE PARK BY CAR & SHUTTLE

In the eastern section of Yosemite Valley, two words pertain—*shuttle bus*. The only reasons to use your private vehicle are to enter and to exit.

Elsewhere in the park, however, a vehicle is more appropriate. If you want to explore Wawona or Tuolumne, hike near Tenaya Lake, or check out Mariposa Grove, having your car is convenient because there is currently no direct bus service from the valley to these destinations. So unless the National Park Service develops a transportation system that reaches beyond the valley walls, automobile travel will remain necessary. If you want to leave most of the driving to others, though, some sample package tours are described below, or you can inquire at tour desks in Yosemite Village, the Ahwahnee, Yosemite Lodge, or Curry Village.

> **ⓣ Tips   Taking Aim at Traffic**
>
> An estimated 7,000 cars enter Yosemite National Park on any given day, leaving many visitors mired in traffic jams. To help ease the traffic volume, an in-park bus system has been in operation for nearly a decade. The project, a joint effort between the National Park Service and the Yosemite Area Regional Transportation System (YARTS), shuttles visitors into Yosemite from nearby communities and commuter lots along the three highways leading into the park. Although it is still a bit early to claim success, park officials are optimistic about the project's ability to help manage Yosemite's traffic problems, thereby providing all visitors with a better and more satisfying experience.

6 ORGANIZED TOURS & RANGER PROGRAMS

The park offers a number of **ranger-guided walks, hikes, and other programs.** Check at one of the visitor centers or in *Yosemite Guide* for current topics, start times, and locations. Walks may vary from week to week, but you can always count on nature hikes, evening discussions on park anomalies (floods, fires, or critters), and the sunrise photography program aimed at replicating some of Ansel Adams's works. The sunrise photo walk always gets rave reviews from the early risers who venture out at dawn. All photo walks require advance registration (get details at the visitor centers). The living-history evening program outside at Yosemite Lodge is great for young and old alike.

Several organizations also host guided trips. Both the **Evergreen Lodge** and the **Yosemite Bug** (see "Lodging" in chapter 5) offer tours of the park; the latter operates van tours as well as backpacking and hiking excursions. Also check out **Incredible Adventures** (ⓒ **800/777-8464;** www.incadventures.com), which offers day tours of Yosemite from San Francisco. **Southern Yosemite Mountain Guides** (ⓒ **800/231-4575;** www.symg.com) runs hiking, backpacking, fishing, and rock-climbing trips.

Yosemite Sightseeing Tours (© 559/658-8687; www.yosemite **47**
tours.com) conducts scheduled tours as well as customized trips.
Costs run about $75 for adults, $65 for teens 13 to 17, and free for
kids 12 and under. Tours are operated on small air-conditioned buses
with huge picture windows. The sightseeing destinations include
Mariposa Grove, Yosemite Valley, and Glacier Point. Geology, flora,
and fauna are pointed out along the way. Stops are scheduled for
lunch, shopping, and photo opportunities. Pickup can be arranged
from various motels throughout Oakhurst and Bass Lake.

A variety of **guided bus tours** is also available. You can buy tickets
at tour desks at Yosemite Lodge, the Ahwahnee, Curry Village, or
beside the Village Store in Yosemite Village. Advance reservations are
suggested for all tours; space can be reserved in person or by phone
(© **209/372-4386**). Always double-check at tour desks for updated
departure schedules and prices. Most tours depart from Yosemite
Lodge, the Ahwahnee, or Curry Village, and adult prices range from
$25 for a 2-hour tour to $92 for a full-day trip with lunch. Children's
rates are usually half that, and discounts are offered for seniors.

The 2-hour **Valley Floor Tour** is a great way to get acclimated to
the park, providing a good selection of photo ops, including El
Capitan, Tunnel View, and Half Dome. This ride is also available on
nights when the moon is full or near full. It's an eerie but beautiful
scene when moonlight illuminates the valley's granite walls and gives
visitors a rare picture of Yosemite. Blankets and hot cocoa are provided. Dress warmly, though, because it can get mighty chilly after the
sun goes down.

The **Glacier Point Tour** is a 4-hour scenic bus ride through the
valley to Glacier Point. Tours also depart from Yosemite Valley to
Tuolumne Meadows. The **Mariposa Grove** trip takes 8 hours and is
especially popular with hikers who want to explore the high country
without relocating their camp from the valley floor.

If you're staying in the valley, the **National Park Service** and **DNC
Parks & Resorts at Yosemite** present evening programs on the park's
history and culture. Past summer programs have included discussions
on early expeditions to Yosemite, the park's flora and fauna, geology,
global ecology, and the legends of the American Indians who once
lived here. Other programs have focused on Mark Wellman's coura-
geous climb of El Capitan—he made the ascent as a paraplegic—and
major threats to Yosemite's environment. Inquire about current programs upon check-in at your hotel or at the information booth outside the visitor center. Although most programs are held in the valley,
a few campgrounds offer campfire programs in the summer.

Spring through fall, the **Yosemite Theater** offers inexpensive theatrical and musical programs designed to supplement Park Service programs. They tend to repeat from year to year, but old favorites include a conversation with noted John Muir impersonator Lee Stetson, a film on Yosemite's future, and singalongs.

4

Hikes & Other Outdoor Pursuits in Yosemite

A nature lover's paradise, Yosemite has some of the most beautiful scenery you'll see anywhere, and the best way to experience the park is to get out onto the trails. Park rangers lead walks and hikes, and guided day treks are also available from a number of organizations (see "Organized Tours & Ranger Programs" in chapter 3).

---

1 DAY HIKES & SCENIC WALKS

Below is a selection of day hikes throughout Yosemite National Park. Distances and times are round-trip estimates unless otherwise noted.

IN & NEAR THE VALLEY

Base of Bridalveil Fall   Bridalveil Fall measures 620 feet from top to bottom. In the spring, expect to get wet. This walk is wheelchair accessible with strong assistance. It's a beautiful waterfall, and easy access makes it a favorite.

0.5 miles/30 min. Easy. Drive or walk to the Bridalveil Fall parking area, about 3 miles west of Yosemite Village. Follow trail markers.

Columbia Rock   This hike mirrors the initial ascent of the Upper Yosemite Fall trail (see below), but stops at Columbia Rock, 1,000 feet above the valley. You won't get a valley view, but the sights here are still impressive. The trail is also less likely to get an accumulation of snow because it's on the sunny side of the valley.

2 miles/2–3 hr. Moderate. Use the trail head for Upper Yosemite Fall (see below).

Four-Mile Trail to Glacier Point   This trail climbs 3,200 feet, but efforts will be rewarded with terrific views of Yosemite Valley's north rim. Check on trail conditions before setting out; it's usually closed in winter. The trail ends at Glacier Point. If you'd like to extend the hike, you can continue on to the Panorama Trail (see below), but beware: The combined round-trip distance is 14 miles.

9.6 miles/7–10 hr. Strenuous. The trail head is 1¼ miles from Yosemite Village, at the Four-Mile parking area at the marker post V-18; or take the shuttle bus to the Yosemite Lodge, stop 8, and walk behind the Lodge over the Swinging Bridge to Southeast Dr. The trail head is ¼ mile west.

Half Dome This long, steep trip, which around 1,000 hikers do each summer day, climbs nearly 5,000 feet. From Happy Isles, take the Mist Trail or the John Muir Trail past Vernal and Nevada falls, and up and into Little Yosemite Valley. Leave the John Muir Trail for the Half Dome Trail. Hiking the final 400 feet up the back of Half Dome requires the use of cables installed in the rock; a strong heart is helpful, too. Half Dome has a small level spot on top, at an elevation of 8,800 feet. It's possible to break up this long trip by camping in Little Yosemite Valley. (You'll need a wilderness permit to camp.)

17 miles/10–14 hr. Very strenuous. Happy Isles, shuttle-bus stop 16.

Lower Yosemite Fall Lower Yosemite Fall is a 320-foot section of Yosemite Falls, but it packs the accumulated punch of the entire 2,425-foot waterfall, and from early spring to midsummer you're likely to get wet. You can also take this trip from Yosemite Village by following the path from the Valley Visitor Center to the Lower Yosemite Fall trail head. Add another half-mile, or 40 minutes, each way. This walk is wheelchair accessible with assistance.

1 mile/30 min. Easy. From shuttle-bus stop 6, follow the paved path from the Yosemite Falls parking area to the base of this waterfall.

Mirror Lake This paved trail climbs 60 feet along the west side of Tenaya Creek to the aptly named Mirror Lake, where overhanging rock formations are reflected in the lake's still surface. This trail connects with a delightful 3-mile loop around the lake, which is wheelchair accessible.

2 miles/1 hr. Easy. Shuttle-bus stop 17.

Mist Trail to Vernal Fall ★★★   This hike begins on the famous 211-mile John Muir Trail, a trail that eventually ends on Mount Whitney in Sequoia & Kings Canyon National Parks. From the Happy Isles Bridge, the trail climbs 400 feet to the Vernal Fall Bridge, which offers water and restrooms, as well as a good view of what lies ahead. From this point, you can either take a series of switchbacks along the side of the mountain, or you can ascend the Mist Trail (our preference), which is a steep climb with 500 steps—it's wet, picturesque, and refreshing. The Mist Trail is so named because the spray from the fall drenches anyone who tackles this route, especially in spring. Be warned—it's slick and requires careful placement of your feet. Once you reach the top, you can relax on a series of smooth granite beaches and soak in the cool, refreshing water before hiking back down. You can continue up 1.4 miles to Nevada Fall and leave the crowds behind for a round-trip of 5.8 miles.

3 miles/2–3 hr. Moderate to strenuous. From Happy Isles, shuttle-bus stop 16, walk to the Happy Isles Bridge. Cross the bridge and follow the signs to the trail.

Panorama Trail   From Glacier Point, this trail drops 3,200 feet. At one of its prettiest points, about 1.5 miles from Glacier Point, it crosses Illilouette Fall. The path continues along the Panorama Cliff and eventually winds up at Nevada Fall, where it's a straight descent to Yosemite Valley via the Mist or John Muir trail. You can hike this trail in conjunction with the Four-Mile Trail; it's also possible to take a bus to Glacier Point and hike only one way.

8.5 miles one-way/4–6 hr. one-way. Moderate to strenuous. The hike begins at Glacier Point, at the east end of the parking area.

Upper Yosemite Fall   Climb this 2,700-foot trail and you'll be rewarded with spectacular views from the ledge above the fall. Take it slowly, rest often, and absorb the scenery as you ascend higher and higher above the valley. One mile (and 1,000 ft.!) up, you'll reach Columbia Rock, which offers a good view. The rest of the trail dips and climbs, and you'll get a bit of mist from the fall above. The last quarter-mile is very rocky and steep, with a series of tortuous, seemingly endless switchbacks that ascend through underbrush before opening at a clearing near the top of the fall. But beware—the view here can induce vertigo. After completing the trail, it's a worthwhile walk upstream to see the creek before it takes its half-mile tumble to the valley floor below. Hikers with the proper permits and equipment can stay here overnight (see chapter 5, "Where to Stay & Eat in Yosemite").

7.2 miles/6–8 hr. Strenuous. Shuttle bus to stop 7; the trail head is next to Camp 4 Walk-in Campground, behind Yosemite Lodge.

SOUTH OF THE VALLEY

Chilnualna Falls from Wawona   One of the tallest falls outside Yosemite Valley, Chilnualna cascades down two chutes. The cascade at the bottom is narrower and packs a real punch after a wet winter. A series of switchbacks leads to the top fall. You may be splashed a bit once you reach the falls, but the trail itself is pretty dry.

8.2 miles/6 hr. Moderate to strenuous. From Wawona, take Chilnualna Rd., just north of the Merced River's South Fork, until it dead-ends at "The Redwoods," about 1.3 miles. This is the trail head.

Grizzly Giant   This is the walking alternative to the Mariposa Grove tram tour described in chapter 3. It's a nice stroll to see an impressive tree, and the hike climbs only 400 feet.

1.6 miles/1½ hr. Easy. The trail begins at a sign near the map dispenser at the east end of the Mariposa Grove parking lot.

Mariposa Grove   This hike sounds long, but there's a one-way option in the summer that uses the Wawona shuttle bus for the return trip. The trail climbs through a forest and then ascends the Wawona Dome and Wawona Basin, both of which provide excellent views.

12 miles/1 long day; with shuttle, about half that. Moderate to strenuous. Park at the Wawona Store parking area and walk east ¼ mile to Forest Dr. The trail head is on the right.

Sentinel Dome ★★   At the starting point, you'll be able to see Sentinel Dome on your left. The trail descends slightly; at the first fork, bear right. The way winds through manzanita and pine trees before beginning its ascent. It's a steep scramble to the top of Sentinel Dome, and you have to leave the trail on the north (left) side to clamber up. The view from the top offers a 180-degree panorama of Yosemite Valley, one of the most stunning vistas in a park that's full of them.

2.2 miles/2–3 hr. Moderate. Take Glacier Point Rd. to the Sentinel Dome parking lot, about 3 miles from Glacier Point.

Taft Point   The walk to Taft Point is not demanding, and it crosses a broad meadow dotted by wildflowers in early summer. Near Taft Point, note the deep chasms, known as fissures, in the rock. Some of the cracks are 40 feet long and 20 feet wide at the top and 100 feet deep. The wall of Yosemite actually overhangs the narrow ravine below, and if you carefully peer over the cliff, you'll notice that your head is on the opposite side of a stream running far beneath you. A small pipe railing farther on marks the 6×3-foot Taft Point overlook hanging over Yosemite Valley.

2.2 miles/2 hr. Moderate. The trail head begins at the same point as the hike to Sentinel Dome (see above). At the fork, head left.

Wawona Meadow Loop   This relaxing stroll encircles Wawona Meadow, curving around at its east end and heading back toward the road. It then crosses the highway and winds through forest until it returns to the Wawona Hotel. Some cars still use this road, so keep your eyes and ears open. This trail is also open to pets.

3.5 miles/1½ hr. Easy. Take the dirt road through the Wawona golf course and walk about 50 yards to the trail.

NORTH OF THE VALLEY

Some of the day hikes discussed below can also be done as overnight backpacking trips; see "Exploring the Backcountry," later in this chapter.

Cathedral Lakes ★   These lakes are set in granite bowls cut by glaciers. The peaks and domes around both Lower and Upper Cathedral lakes are well worth the hike. Lower Cathedral Lake is next to

Cathedral Peak and makes a good place to stop for a snack before heading up the hill to enjoy the upper lake.

7 miles/4–6 hr. Moderate. The trail head is off Tioga Rd., at the west end of Tuolumne Meadows, west of Budd Creek.

Cloud's Rest ★ This hike descends through a wooded area, heading toward Sunrise Lakes. Ascend out of Tenaya Canyon and bear right at the junction (watch for the signposts); the vistas will appear almost at once. The sightline to your destination will be clear—a good thing, since the trail is sketchy at this point. The last stretch to the top is a little spooky, with sheer drops on each side, but your perseverance will be amply rewarded with spectacular views of the park's granite domes. Overnight stays (backcountry permit required) offer the added incentive of beautiful sunrises.

14 miles/7 hr. Strenuous. Take CA 120 to Tenaya Lake. The trail begins at the parking area on the east side of the road near the southwest end of the lake.

Dog Lake ★★   This easy climb through forests offers great views of Mount Dana. Dog Lake is warm, shallow, and great for swimming.

2.8 miles/1 hr. Easy. Take CA 120 to the access road for Tuolumne Lodge. Pass the ranger station and park at the parking lot on the left. Walk north (back toward the highway) up an embankment and cross CA 120 to find Dog Lake Trail.

Elizabeth Lake ★★   This popular day hike attracts a slew of people, which can be a bummer, but it's magnificent and beautiful nonetheless—Elizabeth Lake glistens like ice. Don't forget your camera: The route is one long Kodak moment.

4.8 miles/3 hr. Moderate. Take CA 120 to the group camping area of Tuolumne Meadows Campground, where the trail begins.

Gaylor Lakes   This trail begins with a climb, then descends to an alpine lake. It's a particularly pretty hike in summer, when the mountainsides are dotted with wildflowers.

2 miles/3 hr. Moderate. Take CA 120 to Tioga Pass. The trail head is on the northwest side of the road.

Glen Aulin ★★   This hike takes you to an impressive waterfall with grand views along the way. Start by heading across a flat meadow toward Soda Springs and Glen Aulin. The trail is well marked, and signs along the way do a good job of describing the area's history. This was once the old Tioga Road, which was built in 1883 to serve the Great Sierra Mine in Tioga Pass. The walk offers a view of the landmarks of Tuolumne Meadows. Behind you, Lembert Dome rises almost 900 feet above the meadow. About a quarter-mile from the trail head, the road forks; head right up the grassy slope. In less than 500 feet, you'll see a trail that leaves the road on the right and a steel sign that says GLEN AULIN IS 4.7 MILES AHEAD. This is the trail to take. Along the way, you'll pass Fairview Dome, Cathedral Peak, and Unicorn Peak. The crashing noise you'll hear in early to midsummer is Tuolumne Fall, a cascade of water that drops 12 feet, then 40 feet down a series of ledges. From here you can see a nearby High Sierra Camp. There's also a hikers' camp if you want to spend the night.

11 miles/1 long day. Strenuous. Take CA 120 toward Tuolumne Meadows, about 1 mile east of the Tuolumne Meadows Visitor Center and just a few yards east of the bridge over the Tuolumne River. Follow a marked turnoff and take the paved road on your left. The trail head begins about ⅓ mile ahead, at a road that turns right and heads up a hill toward the stables.

Lembert Dome   This hike offers a bird's-eye view of Tuolumne Meadows—a great vista. A well-marked trail leads you to the top of the dome, and from there you'll see the peaks that encircle the valley, plus get good views of this lovely meadow. It's a great place to watch sunrises and sunsets.

2.8 miles/2 hr. Moderate. The trail head is at a parking lot north of CA 120 in Tuolumne Meadows at road marker T-32. Follow the nature trail that starts here and take off at marker no. 2.

Lyell Canyon ★ This section of the John Muir Trail follows the Lyell Fork of the Tuolumne River up an idyllic green canyon to the rocky Donohue Pass, 12 miles from the trail head and over 2,000 feet above it. While this is a good starting point for a backcountry expedition, a shorter hike up Lyell Canyon—say, 3 miles each way—is perfect for a picnic-centered day hike for most any group of hikers. Backpackers can continue from here into the Ansel Adams Wilderness Area; day hikers can loop back through the Vogelsang area.

Up to 12 miles one-way/5 hr. one-way. Easy to strenuous. The trail head is at the Dog Lake parking lot near Tuolumne Meadows Lodge.

May Lake ★★ Winding through forests and granite, this picturesque hike offers ample opportunities to fish, but swimming is not allowed. Located in the center of Yosemite National Park, it is a good jumping-off point for other high-country hikes. There are numerous peaks surrounding the lake, including the 10,855-foot-high Mount Hoffman, which rises behind the lake. There is a High Sierra Camp here, as well as a hikers' camp on the south side of the lake.

2.5 miles/1 hr. Easy. Take CA 120 east past White Wolf; turn off at road marker T-21 and drive 2 miles to the May Lake parking area.

Mono Pass You'll pass some historic cabin sites, then hike down to Walker Lake, and return via the same route. The hike loops into the Inyo National Forest and the Ansel Adams Wilderness and climbs to an elevation of 10,600 feet. There's a stupendous view of Mono Lake from the top of the trail.

8 miles/4–6 hr. Moderate to strenuous. The trail head for this hike is on the south side of CA 120 as you enter the park from Lee Vining. Drive about 1¹/₂ miles from the park entrance to Dana Meadows, where the trail begins on an abandoned road and up alongside Parker Creek Pass.

Mount Dana This climb is an in-your-face reminder that Mount Dana is Yosemite's second-highest peak. The mountain rises 13,053 feet and the trail gains a whopping 3,100 feet in 3 miles. The views at the top are wonderful, and once you catch your breath you can stand upright again and stare at them in awe. You can see Mono Lake from the summit. In summer, wildflowers add to this hike's beauty.

5.8 miles/5 hr. Very strenuous. The trail head is on the southeast side of CA 120 at Tioga Pass.

North Dome   Walk south down the abandoned road toward the Porcupine Creek Campground. A mile past the campground, the trail hits a junction with the Tenaya Creek and Tuolumne Meadows Trail. Pass a junction toward Yosemite Falls and head uphill toward North Dome. The ascent is treacherous because of loose gravel, but from the top you can catch an all-encompassing view of Yosemite Valley, second only to the view from Half Dome.

8.8 miles/5 hr. Moderate. Take CA 120 east to the Porcupine Flat Campground, past White Wolf. About 1 mile past the campground is a sign for Porcupine Creek at a closed road. Park in the designated area.

Polly Dome Lake (Finds)   This hike is easily the road least traveled. The trip to Polly Dome Lake is a breeze and you'll find nary another traveler in sight. There are several lakes beneath Polly Dome that can accommodate camping. The trail fades in and out, so watch for markers. It crosses a rocky area en route, then skirts southeast at a pond located just after the rocky section. Polly Dome Lake is at the base of—you guessed it—Polly Dome, a visual aid to help hikers stay the course.

13 miles/6 hr. Easy to moderate. Take CA 120 past White Wolf to Tenaya Lake. Drive about ¹/₂ mile to a picnic area midway along the lake. The trail head is across the road from the picnic area.

Soda Springs   This trail crosses Tuolumne Meadows, and then crosses Tuolumne River on a wooden bridge. It's peaceful and beautiful, with the sound of the river gurgling along as it winds slowly through the wide expanse of Tuolumne Meadows. The trail leads to a carbonated spring where you can taste the water, though it gets mixed reviews. Parsons Lodge, an activity center, is close by. Also nearby is the historic McCauley Cabin, which is used for employee housing in the summer.

1.5 miles/1 hr. Easy. Two trail heads: The 1st is at a crosswalk just east of the Tuolumne Meadows Visitor Center. The 2nd leaves from a parking lot north of CA 120 at road marker T-32. Follow the gravel road around a locked gate.

Sunrise Lakes   This hike leads through quiet wooded glades while affording occasional glimpses of distant vistas. Look for a sign that says SUNRISE; then follow the level road to Tenaya Creek, cross the creek, and follow the trail to the right. The hike parallels Tenaya Creek for about 0.3 miles, then moves away through a wooded area and climbs gently up a rocky rise. After a while, the trail descends quickly to the outlet of Mildred Lake. Here you'll be able to see Mount Hoffmann, Tuolumne Peak, and Tenaya Canyon. At the halfway mark, the trail passes through a hemlock grove and comes to a junction. Head left (the trail on the right goes toward Cloud's Rest). About 0.3 miles from the junction, you'll reach Lower Sunrise Lake, tucked into the slope of Sunrise Mountain. The trail climbs past Middle Sunrise Lake and continues upward along a cascading creek coming from Upper Sunrise Lake. The trail follows the lake's shore and opens in less than 0.5 miles onto a wide, bare, sandy pass. Before you is the snowcapped Clark Range. The trail begins its descent, sharply switching back and forth in some places. There is a High Sierra Camp and backpackers' camp a short distance above Upper Sunrise Lake.

7 miles/5–8 hr. Moderate to strenuous. Take CA 120 to Tenaya Lake. The trail begins in the parking area on the east side of the road near the southwest end of the lake.

Tioga Lake to Dana Lake   This is a less-crowded alternative to the above hike to Mount Dana. This particular trail doesn't reach the summit of the mountain, although experienced hikers can reach it on the Mount Dana Trail (see above). The trail is not maintained, although it is fairly visible. This area is easily damaged, so be sure to tread lightly. Mount Dana looms large from the lake's shore.

4.6 miles/2 hr. Moderate to strenuous. Take CA 120 to Tioga Lake. The trail head is on the west side of the lake, about a mile east of the pass.

NEAR HETCH HETCHY

Carlon Falls   This trail off the road to Hetch Hetchy takes visitors through a nicely treed river canyon to a year-round waterfall and a picturesque swimming hole.

4.5 miles/2 hr. Easy. From the turnoff to Hetch Hetchy, park immediately after the 1st bridge and take the trail running west of the river.

Wapama Falls   This trail takes you around the shore of Hetch Hetchy from O'Shaughnessy Dam to the powerful Wapama Falls. It is very misty here—be prepared to get drenched. If you continue another 4.2 miles, you make it to another waterfall and popular backpacking destination, Rancheria Falls.

5 miles/2 hr. Moderate. The trail begins at O'Shaughnessy Dam at the end of Hetch Hetchy Rd.

2 EXPLORING THE BACKCOUNTRY

Of the more than three million people who visit Yosemite each year, 95% never leave the valley, but the brave 5% who do so are well rewarded. A wild, lonelier Yosemite awaits just a few miles from the crowds, where you'll find some of the most grandiose landscape in the

Sierra. Most hikers, especially serious backpackers, head into the high country—a backpacking paradise. Tioga Pass via CA 120 is the gateway to the high country. Once through the pass, the high country presents meadows of wildflowers, stark granite domes, and shimmering rivers and lakes.

Most backpackers set out on their own, as we discuss below, but guided backpacking trips (including overnight trips) are also available with **Yosemite Mountaineering** (© 209/372-8344; www.yosemite mountaineering.com), **Southern Yosemite Mountain Guides** (© 800/231-4575; www.symg.com), and **California Alpine Guides** (© 877/686-2546; www.californiaalpineguides.com). Techniques and skills are taught along the way. Meals are included on longer trips. Private excursions are available, as is transportation to and from the trail heads. Gear is available for rent.

A car is much more vital in Yosemite's high country than in the valley. If you don't bring your own vehicle, there is a once-a-day shuttle bus from the valley to Tuolumne Meadows. The bus leaves the valley at 8am and will let you off anywhere along the route. The driver waits in Tuolumne Meadows for 2 hours before heading back to the valley, where the bus arrives at about 4pm. The fare is about $15 one-way, slightly less for those who hop off midway. In addition, the park offers a free summer-only shuttle bus from Olmsted Point to Tioga Pass, with stops at the lodge, campground, and visitor center.

Tuolumne Meadows is a wide, grassy expanse bordered by the Tuolumne River and tall mountains. Several peaks rise high overhead and offer challenging hiking and rock climbing. In spring and mid-summer, the meadow fills with wildflowers and turns an emerald green. Fishing in the river is popular, and a number of hikes begin in the meadows. Facilities include a general store that stocks last-minute hiking supplies, a slew of canvas tent-cabins (often all full in summer), and a restaurant.

In addition to Tuolumne Meadows, **Tenaya Lake,** set in a bowl of granite surrounded by sheer slopes, is a beautiful destination spot en route to the high country. Tenaya Lake offers canoeing, hiking, fishing, and sailing. It's also open to swimming for those who don't mind dunking in the chilly water—it generally remains frigid until late summer. There's ample parking and a picnic area, and many hikes lead from here to the high country. **White Wolf** is midway between the valley and Tuolumne Meadows (west of Tenaya Lake). It offers a campground, canvas tent-cabins, a small store, and a restaurant. The scenery here is less dramatic, but it serves as a starting point for many hikers going into the Hetch Hetchy area. In the winter, this region is accessible only on snowshoes or cross-country skis.

Like any backcountry experience, staying in the high country—or anyplace outside the valley—requires advance planning and, if you're a beginner, a reasonable itinerary. Planning a 5-day excursion your first time out wouldn't be wise. But an overnighter, or 2 nights out, is reasonable, and Yosemite has hikes that can accommodate and reward those who venture—even briefly—off the well-paved path.

In addition, the park has five **High Sierra Camps** that provide food and shelter, allowing hikers to shun heavy backpacking gear with the knowledge that someone a few miles ahead has everything under control. All camps fill quickly via a lottery system, and advance reservations are necessary. The camps—May Lake, Glen Aulin, Vogelsang, Sunrise, and Merced Lake—are situated about a day's walk apart, and each is a sort of rustic resort. Tent-cabins are furnished with steel bunk beds, woodstoves, and a folding table and chairs. Each bed at Tuolumne includes a mattress, three blankets, a comforter, and a pillow, but beds at the other camps have no blankets or comforters—in other words, bring your own bedding. Soap and candles are also provided. Most tents sleep four, but some accommodate only two people. This means you'll often be sharing your tent with strangers, but the camps tend to attract people who rank high on the camaraderie scale, so that's not usually a problem. Breakfast and dinner are served family style in a dining tent. The food is excellent and portions are generous. One dinner meal included pasta, filet mignon, soup and salad, eggplant Parmesan, and cookies. Breakfast is substantial as well. Box lunches are available for an additional charge. All you need to bring is day-hike gear (including plenty of water or a purifier), plus a flashlight, personal toiletries, something to sleep in, a change of underclothes, and bed linen. In spring, trekking poles are also handy for crossing streams.

Camps are open from mid-June to around Labor Day, conditions permitting. Each camp accommodates 30 to 60 guests; demand exceeds supply, so accommodations are assigned by lottery. Applications are accepted from November 1 to November 30. The lottery drawing is held in mid-December, and guests are notified by the end of February. Cancellations are frequent, however, so it's worth a last-minute call to see if space is available. Overnights at the camps cost $146 to $153 per adult and $90 to $94 per child for lodging and meals (breakfast and dinner; sack lunches are available for an extra fee); there are also packages for multiday saddle trips and guided hikes. A meals-only option is available (about $36 per adult, reservations required) if you want to bring your own tent and eat at the camp. For information or to request an application for High Sierra

Camp accommodations, call ✆ **801/559-4909** or visit www.yosemitepark.com.

PREPARING FOR YOUR BACKCOUNTRY TRIP

Be sure to get a detailed topographical map before setting out on any overnight hike. Maps are available at many stores, visitor centers, and ranger stations throughout Yosemite National Park.

PERMITS & FEES　All overnight backpacking stays require a wilderness permit, available by phone, by mail, or in the park. Permits can be reserved 2 days to 4 months in advance and cost $5, plus $5 for each individual on the permit. Reservations are accepted, usually beginning in late winter. Call ✆ **209/372-0740** or write to Wilderness Permits, P.O. Box 545, Yosemite National Park, CA 95389.

If advance planning isn't your style, first-come, first-served permits are available up to 24 hours before your trip. Permit stations are located at the Yosemite Valley Wilderness Center, Wawona Information Station, Big Oak Flat Information Station, Hetch Hetchy Entrance Station, and Tuolumne Meadows Wilderness Center. (Many of these are open in summer only; Badger Pass is the lone winter-only permit station.) Permits for the popular trails, such as those leading to Half Dome, Little Yosemite Valley, and Cloud's Rest, go quickly. Call ✆ **209/372-0200** for permit station locations and hours.

To get a permit, you must provide a name, address, telephone number, the number of people in your party, the method of travel (snowshoe, horse, foot), the number of horses or other pack animals if applicable, start and end dates, start and end trail heads, and principal destination. Include alternative dates and trail heads as well. Do not neglect getting a permit. You may hike for a week and never run into a ranger, but one is guaranteed to show up and ask to see your permit just as you are re-entering civilization.

SPECIAL REGULATIONS & WARNINGS　Campfires are not allowed above 9,600 feet, and everything you take in must be packed out. Bears live in the high country, so stay alert: Backpackers are required to take bear-proof canisters for storing food. They can be rented for $5 a trip (and a $65 deposit on a credit card) at the Yosemite Valley Wilderness Center and several other park locations.

In the summer months, mosquitoes are public enemy number one, so bring plenty of repellent. Also pack sunscreen, since much of Yosemite's high country is on granite, above the tree line. Stay off high peaks during thunderstorms, and don't attempt a climb if it looks as though a storm is rolling in: The peaks are magnets for lightning.

Note that trail heads along Tioga Road are accessible only on snow-shoes or cross-country skis in winter, as the road is usually closed due to snow from November until June.

Chilnualna Lakes/Buena Vista Peak Loop Although rather difficult, this trek is satisfying, as it takes you from a stunning water-fall through meadows and forests to some lovely lakes. The first day's hike is 8 miles, to Chilnualna Falls, one of the park's tallest falls out-side the valley. It's a strenuous climb up. The bottom fall tumbles down a narrow chute, and 50 feet up is yet another fall; the combina-tion can be quite a vision in spring with a strong winter runoff. Above the falls, the trail ascends via switchbacks up a gorge to a junction. One route will lead through forests toward Bridalveil Campground, the other toward Chilnualna Lakes. Take the Chilnualna Lakes route. Just below this junction are several nice places to camp overnight. There are also a number of nearby swimming holes. From here, it's a climb along the headwaters of the creek to a set of high-altitude lakes. About 2.5 miles up is Grouse Lake Creek. This can be a tough cross during high water, and the rock is very slick, so be careful. Head north (left) for about 0.5 miles after the crossing toward Turner Meadows. At the next junction, head right (east) toward Chilnualna Lakes, about 5 miles away. Buena Vista Peak rises above the lakes. Campsites are plentiful in this area. From the lakes, head up into 9,040-foot Buena Vista Pass. At the pass, head south on Buena Vista Trail toward Royal Arch Lake. The next junction goes right (west) toward Johnson, Crescent, and Grouse lakes. After Grouse Lake is the Grouse Lake Creek crossing and the return trail to Chilnualna Falls and the park-ing area.

28 miles/4 days. Moderate to strenuous. Take CA 41 to Wawona in Yosemite National Park. Turn east on Chilnualna Rd. and stay on this road for about 1¹⁄₃ miles until you reach "The Redwoods," where the road ends. This is the trail head.

Ten Lakes Trail The trail is well marked and picturesque, with lots of rocks to climb around on and several lakes for swimming. The trail offers some great fishing for brook and rainbow trout. Mosqui-toes can be a major deterrent here in summer, however. Backpackers camp at the designated campground at May Lake or in an undevel-oped spot at least a quarter-mile from the shore. There are numerous places to camp, so it's best to discuss options with a ranger.

12 miles/2 days. Moderate. On CA 120 east, pass the White Wolf Campground to the trail-head parking lot, just before a bridge and Yosemite Creek sign. The trail head is on the north side of the road.

4

Impressions

Thousands of tired, nerve-shaken, overcivilized people are beginning to find out that going to the mountains is going home; that wilderness is a necessity.

—John Muir

Tuolumne Meadows to Agnew Meadows along the John Muir Trail This high-altitude climb offers visitors a weekend getaway that leaves flatlanders breathless and displays some of the eastern Sierra's most pristine beauty. Be warned—it's a real heart-thumper. You'll trek through Donohue Pass at 11,056 feet. From the pass, it's mostly downhill. Campers should discuss the numerous overnight options with a park ranger before heading out. You can return the way you came, perhaps exploring the Vogelsang area on your way out, continue on the John Muir Trail to Red's Meadow near Mammoth and Devil's Postpile, or loop back into Yosemite over the truly strenuous switchbacks over 12,260-foot Koip Peak Pass.

28 miles/3 days. Strenuous. The trail head begins where the above hike (Ten Lakes Trail) ends, or take CA 120 to Tuolumne Meadows and the Dog Lake trail head parking area for the John Muir/Pacific Crest Trail/Lyell Fork hikes.

Yosemite Creek This hike approaches Yosemite Falls from behind and ends up at the same place as the Upper Yosemite Fall hike described earlier in this chapter, without the steep climb up from the valley floor. After hiking 2 miles, you'll see the Yosemite Creek Campground. Hike through the campground to the Yosemite Falls Trail. In about 0.8 miles, you'll hit another junction. Head left (south) and hike for another 4 miles to Upper Yosemite Fall. The view from here is heart-stopping. The valley looks Lilliputian with its tiny lodges, people, and cars far below. The waterfall is surrounded by slick rock, so be careful, especially in wet conditions; it seems that every year someone slips over the edge into the abyss below. You can hike back the way you came, or head down the path to the valley if you've got a shuttle system set up or someone to take you back to your car. As with all overnight hikes, discuss camping options with a ranger before heading out.

17 miles/1–2 days. Moderate to strenuous. Take CA 120 east past the White Wolf Campground to the trail head, which is just before a bridge sign for Yosemite Creek. The trail head is on the south side of the highway.

Yosemite Valley to Tuolumne Meadows along the John Muir Trail The trail is well marked and heads from the valley floor past Half Dome and then up to Cathedral Peak. Cathedral Lakes are nearby and worth a side trip. Camp at Tuolumne Meadows.

22 miles/2 days. Moderate to strenuous. The trail begins in the valley at the Happy Isles parking area.

SIDE TRIPS FROM HIGH SIERRA CAMPS

Glen Aulin High Sierra Camp to Waterwheel Falls This walk is long and arduous but takes you to six major waterfalls along the Tuolumne. You'll climb about 1,000 feet along open ledges on the river. There's a lot to see, so get an early start. The trail switches along the noisy river, plunges into a forest, and meanders across a meadow. The most notable waterfalls begin about 1.5 miles into the hike and range from long ribbons to 50-foot-long, 20-foot-wide masses of white water. The trail descends through a canyon. Watch for signs to Glen Aulin (about 3½ miles away). You'll see LeConte Fall on your left beyond a few campsites. It cascades in broad, thin sheets of water, some stretching 30 feet wide as they flow down steeply sloping ledges along the river. A half-mile past LeConte is the top of Waterwheel Falls, a set of long, narrow falls that roar through a trough in the ledge to the left of the trail. With enough water and force, some of the water hits the ledge rock with sufficient force to propel it upward and back in a circle, like a pinwheel. Backward water wheels are rare and should not be confused with the upward and forward spinning water wheel of LeConte Fall. You can climb down to and back from Waterwheel Falls—it'll add a steep 0.3 miles to your trip—before returning to Glen Aulin.

7.6 miles/8 hr. Strenuous (but worth it). Cross Conness Creek; the trail head is on your left about 30 ft. ahead.

Sunrise High Sierra Camp to Upper Cathedral Lake Views of the stunning Cathedral Peak are the highlight of this hike. Descend the stone steps to the John Muir Trail along the north side of a meadow. The trail skirts the meadow and crosses several small creeks. Stick to the John Muir Trail, which will bring you to a branch of Cathedral Fork, which has a riverbed lined with rust-colored rocks. After 2 miles, the trail falls away from the creek and toward Columbia Finger, climbing a rocky slope that quickly levels off. You'll see a variety of peaks along the way, and toward the end, when Cathedral Peak comes into view, you'll be surrounded by 2-mile-high pinnacles that somehow escaped the prehistoric glaciers. The trail descends through a meadow, then on to Upper Cathedral Lake. The trek back to camp offers stunning views from the reverse perspective.

10 miles/6–8 hr. Moderate to strenuous. The hike begins next to the dining tent.

Vogelsang High Sierra Camp to Vogelsang Pass   This hike offers broad views of an assortment of peaks. Turn left from the trail where it crosses the creek (just past the intersection of the pass trail and the camp trail), walk 50 feet upstream, and cross the creek. You'll find nothing but spectacular views. The two towers of Vogelsang Peak lie ahead, stretched apart like some enormous saddle. This walk offers views of Vogelsang Lake. The rough slopes of Vogelsang Peak and Vogelsang Pass are straight ahead. A 50-foot-wide pond surrounded by pinkish granite marks the top of the pass. Cross to the north side for one of the most spectacular views in the High Sierra. Walk a few feet more, to the point where the trail begins to descend toward Lewis Creek, and a magnificent panorama will greet you: 12,080-foot Parson's Peak; 12,503-foot Simmons Peak; 12,960-foot Mount Maclure; the wide 12,561-foot Mount Florence; the summits of Clark Range, Triple Divide, and Merced peaks; the aptly named Red and Gray peaks; and Mount Clark. Look down and you'll see the blue-green Bernice Lake.

3 miles/2–3 hr. Moderate to strenuous. The walk begins on the west side of the dining tent and descends to Fletcher Creek.

---

3 OTHER SPORTS & ACTIVITIES

About the only thing you can't do in Yosemite is surf. In addition to sightseeing, Yosemite is a great place to bike, ski, rock climb, fish, and even golf.

BICYCLING   There are 12 miles of designated bike trails in the eastern end of Yosemite Valley, which is the best place to ride since roads and shuttle-bus routes are usually too crowded and dangerous for bicyclists. Children 17 and under are required by law to wear helmets. During the summer, single-speed bikes (and kiddie trailers) can be rented by the hour ($9.50) or the day ($26) at **Curry Village** (© 209/372-8319). Year-round rentals are available at **Yosemite Lodge** (© 209/372-1208). Bike rentals include helmets for all ages.

CROSS-COUNTRY SKIING   The park has more than 350 miles of skiable trails and roads, including 25 miles of machine-groomed track and 90 miles of marked trails in the Badger Pass area. Equipment rentals, lessons (including excellent beginner lessons), and day and overnight ski tours are available from **Badger Pass Cross-Country Center and Ski School** (© 209/372-8444; www.yosemitepark. com).

FISHING   Several species of trout are found in Yosemite's streams. Information is available from the **California State Department of**

Fish and Game (© 559/243-4005; www.dfg.ca.gov). There are also special fishing regulations in Yosemite Valley; get information at the visitor centers.

GOLF There's one golf course in the park plus several others nearby. **Wawona** (© 209/375-6572) sports a 9-hole, par-35 course that alternates between meadows and fairways. Greens fees are $36 to $42 for 18 holes, cart included.

HORSEBACK RIDING Several companies offer guided horseback rides in and just outside the national park, with rates starting at about $60 for 2 hours, $80 for a half-day, and $120 for a full day. **Yosemite Stables** (© 209/372-8348) offers rides from Yosemite Valley, Tuolumne Meadows, and Wawona; it leads multiday pack trips into the backcountry (call for details). **Yosemite Trails Pack Station** (© 559/683-7611; www.yosemitetrails.com) offers rides just south of Wawona, while **Minarets Pack Station** (© 559/868-3405; www. highsierrapackers.org) leads day trips to Yosemite and the Ansel Adams Wilderness.

ICE SKATING The outdoor ice rink at **Curry Village,** with great views of Half Dome and Glacier Point, is open from early November to March, weather permitting. Admission is $8 for adults, $6 for children; skate rental costs $3. Call © 209/372-8319 for current hours.

RAFTING A raft-rental shop is located at **Curry Village** (© 209/ 372-4386). Daily fees are $26 for adults, $16 for children under 13, and include a raft, paddles, mandatory life preservers, and transportation from Sentinel Beach to Curry Village. Be aware that swift currents and cold water can be deadly. Talk with rangers and shop employees before venturing out to be sure the trip you're planning is within your capabilities.

ROCK CLIMBING Yosemite is considered one of the world's premier playgrounds for both experienced rock climbers and wannabes. The **Yosemite Mountaineering School** (© 209/372-8344; www. yosemitemountaineering.com) provides instruction for beginning, intermediate, and advanced climbers in the valley and Tuolumne Meadows, April through October. Classes last from a day to a week; private lessons are available as well. Rates, which include all equipment, vary according to the class or program.

SKIING Yosemite's **Badger Pass Ski Area** (© 209/372-8430; www.yosemitepark.com) is usually open from Thanksgiving to Easter Sunday, weather permitting. This small resort, located 22 miles from Yosemite Valley, was established in 1935. There are 10 runs, rated 35% beginner, 50% intermediate, and 15% advanced, plus a terrain

(Kids) **Especially for Kids**

Many of the activities listed in this section have special programs for children, including rock climbing and ski lessons. In addition, Yosemite offers Little Cub and Junior Ranger programs, plus special walks and activities for kids. See "Family Travel," in the "Specialized Travel Resources" section of chapter 2.

park, with a vertical drop of 800 feet from the highest point of 8,000 feet. There are five lifts—one triple chair, three double chairs, and a cable tow. Full-day lift tickets cost $35 to $42 for adults, $16 to $20 for kids 7 to 12; half-day tickets are $30 to $33 and $16, respectively.

Facilities at the ski area include several casual restaurants; a ski shop; ski repairs; a day lodge; lockers; and an excellent ski school, thanks to "Ski Ambassador" Nic Fiore, a Yosemite ski legend who arrived in the park in 1947 to ski for a season and never left. Fiore became director of the ski school in 1956, and park officials credit him with making Badger Pass what it is today—a family-oriented ski area where generations have learned the art of skiing.

Where to Stay & Eat in Yosemite

There is no lack of choices for accommodations in and near Yosemite National Park. Yosemite Valley is the hub for lodging, dining, and other services within the park, and is usually quite crowded in summer, but it offers the best location—close to Yosemite's main attractions and with easy access to the park's shuttle-bus system.

A more narrow scope of choices is available outside the valley, but still within the park: You can camp at Wawona, Tuolumne Meadows, White Wolf, and a host of other sites; there are privately owned cabins as well.

In addition, there are some delightful (and generally less expensive) accommodations, campgrounds, and restaurants outside the park in the gateway communities of El Portal, Mariposa, Oakhurst, Lee Vining, and Groveland.

---

1 LODGING

INSIDE THE PARK

Lodging within the park is run by **DNC Parks & Resorts at Yosemite.** Rooms can be reserved up to 366 days in advance by calling *©* **801/559-5000** (TTY 559/252-2846), visiting **www.yosemite park.com**, or writing to Yosemite Reservations, 6771 N. Palm Ave., Fresno, CA 93704.

In addition, more than 130 private homes in the park can be rented through the **Redwoods in Yosemite,** P.O. Box 2085, Wawona Station, Yosemite National Park, CA 95389 (*©* **888/225-6666;** www.redwoodsinyosemite.com). Offerings range from cabins to vacation homes, all furnished and equipped with linens, cookware, and dishes. Nightly rates range from $180 for a one-bedroom cabin to $500 or more for a five-bedroom spread; there are usually 3-night minimum stays in summer, 2-night minimums the rest of the year.

The Ahwahnee ★★★ This hotel is fit for a king or queen—and it has hosted both. Queen Elizabeth II slept here, as did U.S. President John F. Kennedy. It's tough to top the Ahwahnee, a six-story concrete-and-stone structure that offers beautiful views from nearly every window. The common rooms feature three fireplaces large enough to stand in, plus overstuffed sofas and chairs that are the perfect spot for reading or playing games after a day of hiking. Regular guest rooms offer a choice of two doubles or one king-size bed, with a couch, plush towels, and snuggly comforters. The Sunroom Suite is a bright pair of rooms in lime and yellow, with floor-to-ceiling French windows that open out onto the valley. The Library Room's rich decor includes a fireplace and walls of books.

Yosemite Valley, Yosemite National Park. ✆ **801/559-5000.** www.yosemitepark. com. 123 units. Reservations required. $408 guest room or cottage; $562–$1,053 2-room suite; from $1,127 3-room suite. AE, DC, DISC, MC, V. Parking available, or take the shuttle bus to stop no. 3. **Amenities:** Restaurant (see "Where to Eat," later in this chapter); bar; babysitting; concierge; outdoor pool; room service; seasonal tennis courts. *In room:* TV, Wi-Fi (free).

Curry Village Curry Village is best known as a mass of more than 300 canvas tents packed tightly together on the valley's south slope. It was founded in 1899 as a cheap lodging option for valley visitors at a mere $2 a day, but guests can kiss those $2 days goodbye. Still, it's an economical place to crash, and it gives you the feel of a camping vacation without the hassle of bringing your own tent. Note that since these tents are basically canvas affairs, and this is bear country, you'll need to lock up all foodstuffs—and anything that bears might think is food, like toothpaste—in bear-proof lockers, which may be a healthy walk from your tent-cabin.

The canvas tents have wood floors, sleep two to four people, and are equipped with beds, bedding, dressers, and electrical outlets; some have propane heaters. Much more substantial and comfortable are Curry Village's 50 or so attractive wood cabins with private bathrooms. There are also 14 wood cabins that, like the tent-cabins, share a large bathhouse, and 18 motel rooms.

Yosemite Valley, Yosemite National Park. ✆ **801/559-5000.** www.yosemitepark. com. 500 units. Reservations suggested. $94 double tent-cabin; $102 double cabin without bathroom; $140 double cabin with bathroom; $179 double motel room. AE, DC, DISC, MC, V. Parking available, or take the shuttle bus to stop no. 13A, 13B, 14, or 20. **Amenities:** 3 dining options (see "Where to Eat," later in this chapter); bikes; children's programs; outdoor pool; Wi-Fi (free). *In room:* No phone.

Housekeeping Camp (Value) A fun, funky place to spend the night, this is the closest thing to camping without pitching a tent. The sites are fence-enclosed, canvas-roofed, cinder-block cabins built on concrete slabs. Each is equipped with a table, cupboard, electrical outlets, shelves, mirror, and lights. The sleeping areas have two single-size bunks and a double bed. There is a grocery store on the premises.

Yosemite Valley, Yosemite National Park. © 801/559-5000. www.yosemitepark. com. 266 units, all with shared restrooms and shower facilities. Reservations required. $79 per site (up to 4 people; $5 per extra person). AE, DC, DISC, MC, V. Closed Nov–Mar. Parking available, or take the shuttle bus to stop no. 12. *In room:* No phone.

Tuolumne Meadows Lodge   This is not a lodge, but rather another group of canvas tent-cabins. Like White Wolf Lodge (see below), these have tables and wood-burning stoves and sleep up to four people. The lodge is smack-dab in the middle of prime hiking territory that's less crowded than the valley below, though there is still a fair amount of foot and car traffic here. This is also home base for wilderness trekkers and backcountry campers. Facilities include a tour desk, small general store and mountaineering store, gas station, post office, and stables.

Tioga Rd., Tuolumne Meadows, Yosemite National Park. © 801/559-5000. www. yosemitepark.com. 69 canvas tent-cabins, all with shared restrooms and shower facilities. $93 double. Additional $10 per extra adult or $6 per extra child. AE, DC, DISC, MC, V. Parking available in an adjacent lot. Closed in winter. From Yosemite Valley, take CA 120 east 60 miles (about 1½ hr.) toward Tioga Pass. **Amenities:** Restaurant (see "Where to Eat," later in this chapter). *In room:* No phone.

Wawona Hotel ★★   This is a classic Victorian-style hotel that comprises six stately white buildings set near towering trees in a green clearing. The main building was constructed in 1879. Don't be surprised if a horse and buggy rounds the driveway by the fishpond—it's that kind of place. What makes it so wonderful? Maybe it's the wide porches, the nearby 9-hole golf course, or the vines of hops cascading from one veranda to the next. The entire place was designated a National Historic Landmark in 1987. Guest rooms are comfortable and quaint; Clark Cottage (dating back to 1876) is the most intimate. Check out the whistling maintenance man who hits every high note in the "Star-Spangled Banner" while the American flag is hoisted each morning, leaving many bystanders speechless as more than a few Wawona employees chime in to create a veritable whistling orchestra.

Wawona Rd., Wawona, Yosemite National Park. © 801/559-5000. www.yosemite park.com. 104 units (54 with shared bathroom). $145 double with shared bathroom; $217 double with private bathroom. Additional $13–$21 for extra adults. AE, DC, DISC, MC, V. From Yosemite Valley, take CA 41 south 27 miles toward Fresno. **Amenities:** Restaurant (see "Where to Eat," later in this chapter); lounge; golf course; large outdoor pool; outdoor tennis court. *In room:* No phone.

White Wolf Lodge Ⓕinds   Imagine a smaller, quieter, cleaner Curry Village with larger tents, each equipped with a wood-burning stove. White Wolf Lodge is not a lodge per se, but a cluster of canvas tent-cabins, with a few wooden cabins out front. This small outpost was bypassed when Tioga Road was rebuilt. It's halfway between the valley and the high country, and generally isn't overrun with visitors. It's a popular spot for midweek hikers and weekend stopovers. Although it can get crowded, it still retains a homey feeling. Maybe it's the fact that there's no electricity from 11pm to 6am, when the generator is shut off.

The wood cabins all have private bathrooms and resemble regular motel rooms, with neat little porches and chairs out front. The canvas cabins beat the Curry Village style by a mile. Each sleeps four in a combination of twin and double beds. All have tables, and the helpful staff will show guests how to work the wood-burning stoves.

Tioga Rd., White Wolf, Yosemite National Park. © **801/559-5000.** www.yosemite park.com. 24 canvas tent-cabins, 4 wood cabins. All canvas cabins share restrooms and shower facilities. $84–$96 double. Additional $10 per extra adult and $6 per extra child. AE, DC, DISC, MC, V. Parking available across a 2-lane road. Closed in winter. From Yosemite Valley, take CA 120 east 33 miles toward Tioga Pass. **Amenities:** Restaurant (see "Where to Eat," later in this chapter). *In room:* No phone.

Yosemite Lodge at the Falls ★ (Kids)

These comfortable and clean rooms are popular thanks to the lodge's location, with some units offering views of Upper Yosemite Fall. Most units have balconies or patios. It's not uncommon to see deer and other wildlife scampering through this area. Spring mornings bring a wonderful orchestra of songbirds and stunning views at sunrise.

Yosemite Valley, Yosemite National Park. © **801/559-5000.** www.yosemitepark. com. 245 units. Reservations suggested. $179–$207 double. Additional $7–$10 per extra adult. Lower rates Nov–Mar. AE, DC, DISC, MC, V. Parking available, or take the shuttle bus to stop no. 8. **Amenities:** 2 restaurants (see "Where to Eat," later in this chapter); ice-cream stand; lounge; babysitting; bikes; children's programs; large outdoor pool; Wi-Fi (free). *In room:* TV.

Yosemite West Lodging

Pretend you're more than just a temporary visitor: For the unforgettable experience of living in Yosemite National Park (if only for a few nights), what could be better than renting a private home, cottage, or condo unit located right in the park? Yosemite West rents a variety of accommodations, ranging from fairly simple rooms with one queen-size bed and a kitchenette, suitable for one or two people, to spacious vacation homes with full kitchen, two bathrooms, living room, and beds for up to eight. Kitchens and kitchenettes are fully equipped, all bedding is provided, TVs and VCR/DVD players are on hand, and there are even outdoor decks. All units also have automatic or wood-burning fireplaces and charcoal grills. The homes are in a forested area about 10 miles from Yosemite Valley and 8 miles from Badger Pass.

Yosemite National Park. 📞 **559/642-2211**. www.yosemitewestreservations.com. A fluctuating number of privately owned cottages and homes. $95–$295 double. Lower rates early Sept to mid-Dec and early Jan to early May. Credit card policy varies by homeowner. Take CA 41 for 12 miles north of Wawona. *In room:* TV/VCR/DVD player, fridge, kitchen.

OUTSIDE THE PARK

Outside the park you'll find a plethora of choices, many of which are less expensive than lodging within the park.

Along California 120 (West of the Park)

Yosemite Lodgings (www.staynearyosemite.com) is a group of a dozen inns, cabin resorts, and historic hotels near the Big Oak Flat Entrance.

Evergreen Lodge ★★ (**Finds**)   A rough-and-tumble Prohibition-era destination for the workers who built the dam that flooded nearby Hetch Hetchy Valley, Evergreen Lodge has been reborn as one of the best cabin resorts in the Sierra Nevada. Located 7 miles from the roar of the highway, the lodge underwent a major renovation beginning in 2004, when new ownership took over and built new cabins and renovated others. The end results are tremendous: rustic art made from peach boxes, rockers on the decks and porches, a fresh and comfortable feel, and space for two to six guests per cabin. (Also available: "Custom Camping" sites, with tents furnished with cushy foam mattresses and all the necessary gear.) The lodge's excellent recreation program includes guided bike rides and hikes, live music, basket-weaving and dancing classes, and s'mores on the campfire. The restaurant is also top-notch, and the original woodsy bar a classic.

33160 Evergreen Rd., Groveland, CA 95321. 📞 **800/935-6343** or 209/379-2606. www.evergreenlodge.com. 88 units, plus 15 Custom Camping sites. $89–$269 double; $65 campsite. AE, DISC, MC, V. **Amenities:** Restaurant (American); bar; bikes; Wi-Fi (sporadic, free). *In room:* Fridge, no phone.

Groveland Hotel ★★   Owners Peggy and Grover Mosley have poured their hearts into this standout hotel. The building stood vacant for years until the Mosleys decided to forgo a quiet retirement to renovate and reopen the hotel. They've done a great job—the Groveland is now a National Historic Landmark. The hotel consists of two buildings, one constructed in 1849 to house gold miners and the other built in 1914 for workers constructing the dam in Hetch Hetchy Valley. Standard rooms are spacious, with feather beds, antiques, down comforters, and plush robes. Suites have large spa tubs and fireplaces. Many rooms are named after women of the Sierra and local characters, although Lyle's Room honors the hotel's resident ghost. Then there's Charlie's Room, named for a hard-driving, tobacco-spitting stagecoach driver and farmer. When he died, the townspeople learned that he was a she.

18767 CA 120, Groveland, CA 95321. © **800/273-3314** or 209/962-4000. Fax 209/962-6674. www.groveland.com. 17 units, including 3 suites. $145–$185 double; $235–$285 suite. Extra person $25. Rates include buffet breakfast. AE, DC, DISC, MC, V. Pets accepted ($15/night). **Amenities:** Restaurant (see Cellar Door in "Where to Eat," later in this chapter); lounge; room service. *In room:* A/C, TV, hair dryer, MP3 docking station, Wi-Fi (free).

Hotel Charlotte ★ Walking into the Charlotte is like stepping back in time. Built in 1918 by an Italian immigrant of the same name, it's warm, comfortable, and a good choice for those who enjoy the ambience of small historic hotels. Cheerily wallpapered and wainscoted, the guest rooms are small, quaint, and nicely maintained. Several units adjoin each other and have connecting bathrooms (perfect for families) with claw-foot tub/shower combos. The pancake buffet breakfast is great—you can get your fill of coffee, cereals, fruit, juices, flapjacks, and scrambled eggs.

18736 CA 120, Groveland, CA 95321. © **800/961-7799** or 209/962-6455. Fax 209/962-6254. www.hotelcharlotte.com. 10 units, seven 2- to 6-bedroom vacation homes in Groveland. $98–$149 double; $159–$649 vacation home. Rates include full breakfast. AE, MC, V. **Amenities:** Excellent restaurant (see Café Charlotte in "Where to Eat," later in this chapter). *In room:* A/C, TV, Wi-Fi (free).

Sunset Inn ★ (Finds) Just 2 miles from Yosemite's entrance gates, the Sunset Inn is the perfect antidote to the hubbub you encounter in the valley. Surrounded by old-growth forest, the inn's 2 acres were once a bustling logging camp, then became a tourist camp, and now feel a world apart, complete with a frog pond, chicken coop, and hiking trails in every direction. The three cabins here are not new by any means, but have been lovingly restored by Bill Nickell, the carpenter-innkeeper who owns and operates the place with his wife, Lauren. (They've called the property home since the 1970s.) Each cabin has attractive woodwork, quilts, a wood-burning or gas stove, and a full kitchen. The comfy interiors are matched outside, where you'll find picnic tables, barbecue grills, and porches that are ideal for watching the phenomenon from which the inn takes its name. The Nickells also manage a pair of homes a few miles west.

33569 Harden Flat Rd., Groveland, CA 95321. © **888/962-4360** or 209/962-4360. www.sunsetinn-yosemitecabins.com. 3 cabins, 2 vacation homes. $140–$230 cabin; $250–$400 vacation home. AE, MC, V. *In room:* Kitchen, Wi-Fi (free).

Yosemite Rose ★ Situated on 210 acres of working ranchland, this beautiful Victorian B&B is actually a product of the 21st century: Built in 2000, the inn was modeled after the Mountain View, California, home of Henry Rengstorff, the 19th-century owner of the spot now known as Silicon Valley. From the public rooms (featuring a pool table, murals, and a player piano) to the grounds (with a stocked fishing pond, stables, and an olive orchard) to the rooms (with top-end soft goods and compelling antiques), innkeeper Katherine Davalle has left little to chance. A good many of the furnishings here have amazing stories behind them: The Scelestia Room's antique Danish headboard has the face of a demon in the grain, and the bedstead in the cottage was brought in on a settler's wagon.

22830 Ferretti Rd., Groveland, CA 95321. © **866/962-6548.** Fax 209/962-7750. www.yosemiterose.com. 7 rooms, including 1 suite, plus 1 cottage. $161 double; $185 suite; $220 cottage. Rates include full breakfast. AE, DISC, MC, V. *In room:* A/C, kitchen, no phone, Wi-Fi (free).

Along California 140

Mariposa Lodge Three generations of the Gloor family have run this reliable and well-maintained motel on Mariposa's main drag for over 30 years, and their standards are surprisingly high. The place has grown over the years from one building to three, with smaller rooms in the original structure, and larger rooms in the newer two. The most spacious have mission decor and impressive vanities; many also have private balconies. Landscaping is superlative for a roadside motel, especially the garden courtyard around the pool.

5052 CA 140 (P.O. Box 733), Mariposa, CA 95338. © **800/966-8819** or 209/966-3607. www.mariposalodge.com. Fax 209/742-7038. 45 units. $59–$129 double. AE, DISC, MC, V. **Amenities:** Jacuzzi; outdoor pool. *In room:* A/C, TV, fridge, Wi-Fi (free).

Poppy Hill Bed & Breakfast ★ This restored country farmhouse, surrounded by large oak and pine trees, provides a delightful escape from the hustle and bustle of the developed areas of the park and nearby gateway communities. The inn is decorated with a variety of antiques, most from the 1800s, but also including "new" furnishings such as the 1925 Wurlitzer baby-grand piano in the parlor. Each of the attractive bedrooms declares its individual decor in its name—Mariposa Lily, Iris, Willow, and, of course, Poppy. All have down comforters, robes, and antique furnishings. Outside, a large rolling lawn is punctuated by flower gardens—one hillside bursts into color when the poppies bloom in spring. The second-floor balcony overlooks an ancient spreading oak tree, which entices the birds to entertain you while you relax in quietude. Breakfast is a big event, with such entrees as eggs picante, puffed apple pancakes, or croissant French toast.

5218 Crystal Aire Dr., Mariposa, CA 95338. © **800/587-6779** or 209/742-6273. www.poppyhill.com. 4 units. $125–$150 double. Rates include full breakfast. AE, DC, DISC, MC, V. Take CA 140 east out of Mariposa (toward Yosemite National Park) 3 miles, turn left on E. Whitlock Rd., go for 1¼ miles, turn right onto Crystal Aire Dr., and go ⅛ mile to the B&B. **Amenities:** Outdoor Jacuzzi. *In room:* A/C, no phone.

River Rock Inn (Value) Mariposa's oldest motel (dating back to 1941) recently received a much-needed update that transformed it from a roadside has-been to a bright and cheery boutique motel. Each of the small rooms has been uniquely decorated and is now comfortably chic. At the Deli Garden Cafe, guests enjoy breakfasts of pastries, fresh fruit, and strong coffee.

4993 7th St., Mariposa, CA 95338. (© **209/966-5793.** www.riverrockncafe.com. 7 units. $79–$95 double. Rates include continental breakfast. AE, MC, V. **Amenities:** Restaurant. *In room:* A/C, TV, fridge (in some), no phone.

Yosemite Bug Rustic Mountain Resort & Spa ★ (Finds) The Yosemite Bug started as a hostel in 1996, but it grew and grew, and is now much, much more. The place has something for everybody, with accommodations that range from dorm rooms and tent-cabins to delightful private rooms, plus a good restaurant, a spa, and loads of personality. Surrounded by forest, most of the units have woodsy views that will make you feel like you're in the national park. The dorm rooms are basic, with bunk beds, heat, air-conditioning, individual lockable storage boxes, and conveniently located communal bathrooms and kitchen. The tent-cabins have wooden floors and framing, no heat, and various bed combinations, including family units with one double and two single beds. Private rooms have themes, from Western to hippie. The Yosemite Bug is along the route for the YARTS bus into Yosemite National Park and also offers transportation and tours on the Bug Bus (www.yosemitebugbus.com). Perhaps the best feature of all is the idyllic swimming hole right down the slope from the main lodge, especially on those dog days of summer.

6979 CA 140 (P.O. Box 81), Midpines, CA 95345. (© **866/826-7108** or 209/966-6666. Fax 209/966-9667. www.yosemitebug.com. 67 hostel beds, 14 private rooms with private bathroom, 8 private rooms with shared bathroom, 16 tent-cabins, 1 studio, 1 private house. Hostel beds $22–$25 per person; private room with bathroom $75–$125 for 2–5 people; private room with shared bathroom $50–$90 for 2–5 people; tent-cabin $30–$55; studio/private house $125–$300. AE, DISC, MC, V. **Amenities:** Restaurant (see Cafe at the Bug In "Where to Eat," later in this chapter); Jacuzzi; sauna; spa; Wi-Fi (free). *In room:* No phone.

Yosemite View Lodge ★ Just outside the park's Arch Rock Entrance, this lodge offers nice accommodations on the Merced River. A number of the rooms are brand-new or recently refurbished, and many feature fireplaces, private decks or patios, kitchenettes, and spa tubs and showers for two.

The Yosemite View's sister property, the **Yosemite Cedar Lodge,** is just 15 miles down the road, with similar accommodations and rates. Just beyond the Cedar Lodge is **Yosemite Resort Homes,** at the historic Savage's Trading Post, featuring newly renovated, fully equipped vacation abodes that sleep up to 12 with rates of $300 to $600 a night.

11136 CA 140 (P.O. Box D), El Portal, CA 95318. ℂ **800/321-5261** or 209/379-2681. Fax 209/379-2704. www.yosemiteresorts.us. 335 units. $95–$194 double; $155–$450 suite. AE, MC, V. **Amenities:** 2 restaurants; lounge; 5 outdoor Jacuzzis and 1 indoor whirlpool; 3 outdoor pools and 1 indoor pool. *In room:* A/C, TV, kitchenette (most rooms).

Along California 41

Château du Sureau & Spa ★★★ One of the standout B&Bs in all of California, the lavish Château du Sureau is as close as you can get to Europe on this side of the Atlantic. A world away from the rest of Oakhurst, the 9,000-square-foot inn has an elegant, near-magical ambience. Its stylish, uniquely decorated accommodations include the extraordinary Saffron Room, with a king-size ebony-and-ivory bedroom set from 1834, and the Sweet Geranium Room, with a private balcony overlooking sumptuous gardens. There are details both time-tested (fresh fruit and fireplaces) and modern (CD players), plus scads of impressive art pieces around every corner. The grounds here are similarly phenomenal—featuring a new spa, a bocce court, and a lawn-size chessboard with 3-foot-high pawns—and the restaurant, Erna's Elderberry House, is simply sublime.

48688 Victoria Lane (P.O. Box 577), Oakhurst, CA 93644. ℂ **559/683-6860.** Fax 559/683-0800. www.chateausureau.com. 11 units, including 1 private house. $385–$585 double; $2,950 guesthouse. Rates include full breakfast. AE, MC, V. **Amenities:** Restaurant (see Erna's Elderberry House in "Where to Eat," later in this chapter); outdoor pool; spa. *In room:* A/C, CD player, no phone, Wi-Fi (free).

The Homestead ★ Secluded on 160 acres of woodland with plenty of trails, this off-the-beaten-path establishment is a gem. The delightful cottages here are rustic yet modern, with four-poster log beds, Saltillo tile floors, stone fireplaces, and separate sitting and dining areas, plus the conveniences of TVs, satellite radio, and air-conditioning. Each unit has its own unique bent, from the romantic Garden Cottage to the cozy Star Gazing Loft to the two-bedroom Ranch House (the most family-friendly option here). Smoking is not allowed.

41110 Rd. 600, Ahwahnee, CA 93601. ℂ **559/683-0495.** Fax 559/683-8165. www. homesteadcottages.com. 5 cottages, 1 house. $145–$219 double; $349–$374 house. AE, DISC, MC, V. Drive 4½ miles north of Oakhurst on CA 49, then south on Rd. 600 for 2½ miles. *In room:* A/C, TV, hair dryer, Internet (free), kitchen, no phone.

Hounds Tooth Inn ★ With a Victorian look despite its 1997 origins, the Hounds Tooth is a good choice for those who want easy access to Yosemite from the south side, but desire more intimacy than a motel or sprawling resort can offer. Set a few hundred feet from the highway, the off-white inn houses a dozen similar guest rooms, each with modern conveniences as well as antique reproductions and in-room sinks. There's also a private summer house (850 sq. ft.) with a king-size bed, kitchenette, Jacuzzi, and private patio. The garden area is something of a work of art, perfect for whiling away an evening in peace and quiet. Smoking is not allowed.

42971 CA 41, Oakhurst, CA 93644. (✆ **888/642-6610** or 559/642-6600. Fax 559/658-2946. www.houndstoothinn.com. 13 units, including 1 cottage. $95–$199 double; $225 cottage. AE, DC, DISC, MC, V. *In room:* A/C, TV/VCR, hair dryer, kitchenette, Wi-Fi (most rooms, free).

Tenaya Lodge at Yosemite ★   The top-rated Tenaya Lodge seems to have one foot in the Adirondack Mountains and another in the Southwest. This three- and four-story resort is set on 35 acres surrounded by Sierra National Forest, and it features a full slate of organized recreational activities. The comfortable guest rooms are modern, and the grand lobby has an impressive river-rock fireplace that towers three stories. In 2008, the lodge acquired the adjacent Apple Tree Inn and renovated its 53 basic cottages. Tenaya Lodge is an especially cozy choice for winter visitors.

1122 CA 41, Fish Camp, CA 93623. (✆ **800/635-5807** or 559/683-6555. Fax 559/683-0249. www.tenayalodge.com. 297 units, including 20 suites and 53 cottages. $155–$379 double; $375–$719 suite; $250–$450 cottage. Children stay free in parent's room. Buffet breakfast $30 per couple. AE, DC, DISC, MC, V. **Amenities:** 5 restaurants; health club; indoor and outdoor pools; room service. *In room:* A/C, TV, hair dryer, Wi-Fi ($10/day).

Along U.S. 395 (Lee Vining)

El Mono Motel ★   Built in the 1920s, this artfully renovated European-style lodging is our pick on the east side of the park in Lee Vining. Fronted by attractive porches and a barbecue area, the guest rooms feature vibrant color schemes and down comforters; the only drawbacks are their small size and the fact that some of them share bathrooms. But all in all, this eclectic lodging is a perfect place to bunk after an expedition in Tuolumne Meadows. The property is also home to a good deal of local art, a coffeehouse, and an organic garden.

51 U.S. 395, Lee Vining, CA 93541. (✆ **760/647-6310.** www.elmonomotel.com. 11 units (6 with shared bathroom). $60–$92 double. Closed Nov to late Apr. MC, V. **Amenities:** Restaurant. *In room:* A/C, TV, no phone, Wi-Fi (free).

Lake View Lodge ★   Spread across several green lawns populated by birds and butterflies, this former chain property is now a first-rate independent. The reliably clean, well-maintained rooms and cottages are set off from the main highway.

51285 U.S. 395, Lee Vining, CA 93541. ℭ **800/990-6614.** www.lakeviewlodge yosemite.com. 53 units, including 7 cottages. $89–$134 double; $89–$209 cottage. AE, DISC, MC, V. **Amenities:** Wi-Fi (free). *In room:* A/C (fans in cottages), TV, fridge (most rooms).

2 CAMPING

There are numerous camping opportunities both within and surrounding Yosemite National Park. Brief descriptions of individual campgrounds follow; you'll find additional details in the campground chart on p. 82.

Note: When camping in this area, proper food storage (bear-proof canisters or lockers) is *required* for the sake of the black bears in the parks, as well as for your safety. See local bulletin boards for instructions.

INSIDE THE PARK

First, the bad news: Yosemite Valley lost half of its roughly 800 campsites during a flood in early 1997. The lost campsites will eventually be replaced somewhere outside of the Merced's flood plain, but no one knows exactly when or where this will happen. Therefore, campsite reservations are a really good idea. Reservations are accepted beginning on the 15th of each month and can be made up to 5 months in advance; make your reservations (ℭ **877/444-6777;** www. recreation.gov) as soon as possible, especially for sites in the valley. Unless noted otherwise, pets are accepted in all of the following campgrounds. Additional campground information is available by touch-tone phone at ℭ **209/372-0200.**

Wilderness permits are required for all overnight backpacking trips in the park, whether you decide to use an established campsite or pick out your own camping area. No wilderness camping is allowed in the valley. For more information on wilderness camping, including Yosemite's High Sierra Camps, see chapter 4, "Hikes & Other Outdoor Pursuits in Yosemite."

The busiest campgrounds in the park are in Yosemite Valley. All four of the following campgrounds are in the valley and have flush toilets and access to the showers nearby at Camp Curry ($2). **Upper Pines Campground** is pretty and shady, but you won't find peace and quiet here in the summer. Parking is available, or you can take the shuttle bus to stop no. 15 or 19. **Lower Pines Campground** is wide open with lots of shade, but limited privacy. Still, it's a nice place with clean bathrooms, and it's bordered on the north by a picturesque meadow. Parking is available, or take the shuttle bus to stop no. 19.

North Pines Campground ★ is beautifully situated beneath a grove of pine trees that offers lots of shade but little privacy. The campground is near the river, roughly a mile from Mirror Lake. Parking is available, or take the shuttle bus to stop no. 18. Reservations are required for Upper, Lower, and North Pines campgrounds. **Camp 4** (also called Sunnyside Walk-In) has tent sites only. It's a small campground that's become a magnet for hikers and climbers taking off or returning from trips. It's situated behind Yosemite Lodge, near the trail head for Yosemite Falls, and close to rocks frequently used by novice rock climbers. Pets are not permitted. Parking is available about 150 feet away, or take the shuttle bus to stop no. 7.

Elsewhere in the park, **Bridalveil Creek Campground,** at Glacier Point, is set along Bridalveil Creek, which flows to Bridalveil Fall—a beauty of a waterfall, especially after a snowy winter or wet spring. Located near beautiful Glacier Point, and featuring flush toilets, this campground is away from the valley crowds but still within a moderate drive to the valley sights. The campground can accommodate some pack animals; call for information. Take CA 41 (from either direction) to Glacier Point Road. The campground is about 8 miles down the road.

Several campgrounds are located in the vicinity of the Big Oak Flat Entrance, roughly 20 to 25 miles from Yosemite Valley. **Hodgdon Meadow Campground,** which has RV and tent sites, including some walk-in sites, requires reservations May through September but is first-come, first-served the rest of the year. It has flush toilets and is located about 1 mile inside the entrance along North Crane Creek and near the Tuolumne River's South Fork. The Big Trees are 3 miles southeast. **Crane Flat Campground,** a large, pleasant campground with flush toilets, is located on Big Oak Flat Road near the Tioga Road turnoff. **Tamarack Flat Campground** is a bit off the beaten path and therefore more secluded than most, which means fewer folks rest their heads here. Equidistant from Yosemite Valley and Tuolumne Meadows, it has pit toilets, does not allow pets, and is not suitable for large RVs or trailers. Take Tioga Road east from Big Oak Flat Road about 3 miles and turn right onto the access road. The campground is another 3 miles down the road.

Options in the White Wolf area include **Porcupine Flat Campground,** which offers lots of shade, shrubs, and trees, although facilities are pretty much limited to pit toilets. You have a chance of finding a spot here if you're in a pinch. Pets are not permitted. It's located near Yosemite Creek along Tioga Road, 16 miles west of Tuolumne Meadows and 38 miles east of Yosemite Valley. **White Wolf Campground,** secluded in a forest, is a generally delightful campground where you might want to spend several days. It has flush toilets and offers easy access to nearby hiking, with trails that lead to several lakes, including Grant Lake and Lukens Lake. On the down side, mosquitoes make their presence felt here in summer. From Big Oak Flat Road, turn east onto Tioga Road, drive 15 miles to White Wolf Road, and turn left. The road dead-ends at the campground.

Among Yosemite's other camping opportunities is **Tuolumne Meadows Campground,** the biggest in the park and, amazingly, often the least crowded. Its location in the high country makes it a good spot from which to head off with a backpack. The site is also near the Tuolumne River, making it a smart choice for anglers. In addition to standard RV/tent sites, the campground has 25 walk-in spaces for backpackers and eight group sites; half of the sites require reservations. There are flush toilets, and showers are available (for a fee) at nearby Tuolumne Lodge. From Big Oak Flat Road, head east on Tioga Road for about 45 miles to Tuolumne Meadows.

Wawona Campground, which requires reservations May through September (but is open year-round), has flush toilets and can accommodate pack animals; call for information. There's not much seclusion here, but the location, shaded beneath towering trees, is beautiful. The campground is near the Mariposa Grove of giant sequoias and is also close to the Merced River, which offers some of the better fishing in the park. The campground is about 1 mile north of Wawona. **Yosemite Creek Campground ★,** in a pretty setting along Yosemite Creek, has pit toilets and little else in terms of facilities, but sometimes has sites available when the park's other campgrounds are full. From Big Oak Flat Road, head east on Tioga Road for about 30 miles and turn right on the access road. The campground is 5 miles down the road.

OUTSIDE THE PARK

Yosemite is surrounded by national forests that offer campgrounds comparable to the ones in the park, although often less developed and less crowded. There are also private campgrounds, which usually provide level sites, complete RV hookups, hot showers, coin-operated laundries, convenience stores, and other amenities.

West Along California 120

The following campgrounds, located along CA 120 west of the park, are all in the Stanislaus National Forest's **Groveland Ranger District,** 24545 CA 120, Groveland, CA 95321 (© **209/962-7825;** www. fs.fed.us/r5/stanislaus/groveland). They all have vault toilets and can accommodate rigs up to 22 feet long.

Yosemite Campgrounds

CAMPGROUND	ELEV. (FT.)	TOTAL SITES	RV HOOKUPS	DUMP STATION	TOILETS	DRINKING WATER	SHOWERS	FIRE PITS/ GRILLS	LAUNDRY	PUBLIC PHONES	RESERVATIONS POSSIBLE	FEES	OPEN
INSIDE YOSEMITE NATIONAL PARK													
Bridalveil Creek	7,200	110	0	No	Yes	Yes	No	Yes	No	Yes	No	$14	July to early Sept
Camp 4	4,000	35	0	No	Yes	Yes	Nearby	Yes	Nearby	Yes	No	$5	All year
Crane Flat	6,191	166	0	No	Yes	Yes	No	Yes	No	Yes	Yes	$20	June–Sept
Hodgdon Meadow	4,872	105	0	No	Yes	Yes	No	Yes	No	Yes	May–Sept	$20	All year
Lower Pines	4,000	60	0	Nearby	Yes	Yes	Nearby	Yes	Nearby	Yes	Yes	$20	Mar–Oct
North Pines	4,000	81	0	Nearby	Yes	Yes	Nearby	Yes	Nearby	Yes	Yes	$20	Apr–Sept
Porcupine Flat	8,100	52	0	No	Yes	No	No	Yes	No	Yes	No	$10	June–Sept
Tamarack Flat	6,315	52	0	No	Yes	No	No	Yes	No	Yes	No	$10	June to early Sept
Tuolumne Meadows	8,600	304	0	Nearby	Yes	Yes	Nearby	Yes	No	Yes	Yes	$20	July–Sept
Upper Pines	4,000	238	0	Yes	Yes	Yes	Nearby	Yes	Nearby	Yes	Yes	$20	All year
Wawona	4,000	93	0	Nearby	Yes	Yes	No	Yes	No	Yes	May–Sept	$20	All year
White Wolf	8,000	74	0	No	Yes	Yes	No	Yes	No	Yes	No	$14	July–Sept
Yosemite Creek	7,659	75	0	No	Yes	No	No	Yes	No	Yes	No	$10	July–Sept

OUTSIDE THE PARK

Big Bend	7,800	17	0	No	Yes	Yes	No	Yes	No	No	$19	Late Apr to mid-Oct
Ellery Lake	9,500	21	0	No	Yes	Yes	No	Yes	No	No	$19	June to mid-Oct
Jerseydale	4,000	10	0	No	Yes	Yes	No	Yes	No	No	Free	May–Nov
Junction	9,600	13	0	No	Yes	No	No	Yes	No	No	$14	June–Oct
Lost Claim	3,100	10	0	No	Yes	Yes	No	Yes	No	No	$14–$28	May to Labor Day
Lumsden	1,500	10	0	No	Yes	No	No	Yes	No	No	Free	All year
Lumsden Bridge	1,500	9	0	No	Yes	No	No	Yes	No	No	Free	Mid-Apr to Oct
The Pines	3,200	11	0	No	Yes	Yes	No	Yes	No	No	$14	All year
Saddlebag Lake	10,000	20	0	No	Yes	Yes	No	Yes	No	No	$17	June to mid-Oct
South Fork	1,500	8	0	No	Yes	No	No	Yes	No	No	Free	Mid-Apr to Oct
Summerdale	5,000	29	0	No	Yes	Yes	No	Yes	Yes	No	$19	June–Nov
Summit	5,800	6	0	No	Yes	No	No	Yes	No	No	Free	June–Oct
Sweetwater	3,000	12	0	No	Yes	Yes	No	Yes	No	No	$17	Apr–Oct
Tioga Lake	9,700	13	0	No	Yes	Yes	No	Yes	No	No	$19	June to mid-Oct
Yosemite–Mariposa KOA	2,400	89	51	Yes	Yes	Yes	Yes	Yes	Yes	A good idea	$40–$50	Mar to mid-Nov

Lumsden Campground is located along the Tuolumne River, on a scenic stretch between the Hetch Hetchy and Don Pedro reservoirs. The campground offers fishing in a primitive setting, but can get unbelievably hot in the summer. From Groveland, take CA 120 about 9 miles east to Ferretti Road, turn left and drive about 1 mile to Lumsden Road, turn right at Lumsden Road, and travel about 5 miles on a steep, narrow dirt road to the campground. Lumsden Bridge Campground is about 1½ miles past Lumsden Campground (on Lumsden Rd.). Set in a pine and oak forest along the Tuolumne River, it is a favorite of rafters because the location is close to some of the Tuolumne River's best (and most scenic) stretches of white water. South Fork Campground, also located along Lumsden Road, near Lumsden and Lumsden Bridge campgrounds, is a pretty spot near the Tuolumne River. It is recommended that trailers or vehicles with low ground clearance not be taken to any of the above three campgrounds.

The Pines Campground is located about 9 miles east of Groveland via CA 120, and although it's in a mixed conifer forest, it can get hot in the summer. Drinking water is available only in the summer. Lost Claim Campground, about 12 miles east of Groveland via CA 120, offers easy access on a paved road. There are some trees and the river is nearby. Drinking water is supplied by a hand pump. Trailers are not recommended. Sweetwater Campground, located 15 miles east of Groveland on CA 120, is a pretty option in a mixed conifer forest with shady sites, but it also gets hot in summer.

Along California 140

Jerseydale Campground, situated in the Sierra National Forest, 1600 Tollhouse Rd., Clovis, CA 93611-0532 (© 559/297-0706; www. fs.fed.us/r5/sierra), provides refuge from the crowds and makes a great base for exploring the area. There are vault toilets and hiking trails, and you can get to the Merced River via a nearby trail head. From Mariposa, drive about 12 miles northwest on CA 49 to Jerseydale Road, which leads to the campground and adjacent Jerseydale Ranger Station.

For those who want all the amenities of a top-notch commercial campground, a good choice is the Yosemite–Mariposa KOA, 6323 CA 140, Midpines, CA 95345 (© 800/562-9391 for reservations, or 209/966-2201; www.koa.com). Located 7 miles northeast of Mariposa and 23 miles from the park entrance, this KOA has pines and oaks that shade many of the sites, a catch-and-release fishing pond, pedal boats (in the summer), a swimming pool, and a playground.

There's also a convenience store and propane for sale. A kids' favorite is the train caboose containing video games. There are also a dozen camping cabins (you share the bathhouse with campers), with rates from $68 to $155.

Along California 41

Two Sierra National Forest campgrounds (see contact information for Jerseydale Campground, above) offer pleasant camping, with vault toilets, in a woodsy atmosphere along CA 41, southwest of Yosemite. **Summerdale Campground** is about a mile north of Fish Camp via CA 41, on the South Fork of the Merced River, and is often full by noon on Fridays; reservations are available through www.recreation.gov. **Summit Campground,** in the Chowchilla Mountains, about 5 miles west of Fish Camp via a Forest Service road, is a little campground that's often overlooked.

East Along California 120

The Inyo National Forest operates a number of small, attractive campgrounds along CA 120 east of the national park. These include **Big Bend Campground,** 7 miles west of Lee Vining via CA 120. Located on the eastern Sierra along Lee Vining Creek, this campground is sparse but breathtaking; it has flush toilets. **Ellery Lake Campground,** which also has flush toilets, is at scenic Ellery Lake, about 9 miles west of Lee Vining via CA 120. **Junction Campground** is near Ellery and Tioga lakes, with easy access to the Tioga Tarns Nature Trail. It has vault toilets and is 10 miles west of Lee Vining along CA 120.

At 10,000 feet, **Saddlebag Lake Campground** is the highest-elevation drive-to campground in the state. It's situated along Saddlebag Lake and near Lee Vining Creek. The campground is a beautiful place that's worth staying at and exploring for a while. It's also a great base for those who want to head out into the wilderness with a backpack. Flush toilets are available. From Lee Vining, drive 10 miles west on CA 120; then turn north on Saddlebag Lake Road and go about 2 miles to the campground. **Tioga Lake Campground,** another high-elevation campground, is a pretty place to camp and has flush toilets. From Lee Vining, drive 10 miles west on CA 120.

Information on these U.S. Forest Service campgrounds is available from the **Mono Basin Scenic Area Visitor Center,** located on the west shore of Mono Lake (P.O. Box 429, Lee Vining, CA 93541; © 760/647-3044), and the **Inyo National Forest,** 351 Pacu Lane, Ste. 200, Bishop, CA 93514 (© **760/873-2400;** www.fs.fed.us/r5/inyo).

3 WHERE TO EAT

There are plenty of dining possibilities in and near the park, so you certainly won't go hungry. However, you won't find many bargains, so be sure to bring a full wallet with your empty stomach.

IN THE VALLEY

The Ahwahnee Dining Room ★★ AMERICAN/CONTINEN-TAL   Even if you're a dyed-in-the-wool, sleep-under-the-stars back-packer, the Ahwahnee Dining Room will not fail to make an impression. This is where the great outdoors meets four-star cuisine, and it's a wonderful place to celebrate a special occasion. The cavern-ous room, its candelabra chandeliers hanging from the 34-foot-high beamed ceiling, seats 350, but feels intimate once you're at your table. The menu changes frequently and offers a good variety of creative yet recognizable dishes, such as pan-roasted Alaskan halibut, bone-in rib-eye, and rack of lamb. An extensive wine list, featuring selections from California and abroad, is offered at lunch and dinner. Breakfast includes egg dishes, hot cakes, and the like, plus specialties such as an apple crepe filled with spiced apples and raspberry purée. Lunch choices include sautéed trout, a grilled portobello sandwich, and a variety of plates and salads. Sunday brunch is a big event. *Note:* The dinner dress code requires men to wear a collared shirt and long pants and women to wear a dress, skirt, or pants with a blouse; no shorts are permitted at any time.

The Ahwahnee, Yosemite Valley. ✆ **209/372-1489.** www.yosemitepark.com. Reservations required for dinner. Breakfast $7–$21; lunch $15–$23; dinner $30–$49; Sun brunch $49 adults, $24 children. AE, DC, DISC, MC, V. Mon–Sat 7–10:30am, 11:30am–3pm, and 5:30–9pm; Sun 7am–3pm and 5:30–9pm. Shuttle-bus stop no. 3.

Curry Village Coffee Corner COFFEE SHOP   Specialty coffees and fresh-baked pastries are the fare here. You can also get ice cream and shakes after 11am.

Curry Village, Yosemite Valley. Most items $1–$4. AE, DC, DISC, MC, V. Summer daily 6am–10pm; winter daily 7am–10pm. Shuttle-bus stop nos. 13A, 13B, 14, and 20.

Curry Village Pavilion Ⓚⁱᵈˢ AMERICAN   A good spot for the very hungry. All-you-can-eat breakfast and dinner buffets offer a wide variety of well-prepared basic American selections at fairly reasonable prices.

Curry Village, Yosemite Valley. Breakfast $9.50 adults, $7.50 children; dinner $12 adults, $10 children. DC, DISC, MC, V. Daily 7–10am and 5:30–8pm. Shuttle-bus stop nos. 13A, 13B, 14, and 20.

| Fun Facts | **Food for Thought** |

DNC Parks & Resorts at Yosemite reports that Yosemite visitors consume over 100,000 gallons of milk, 100,000 hot dogs, 30,000 gallons of ice cream, and 2.5 million cups of coffee annually.

Curry Village Pizza Patio ★ **Kids** PIZZA Need to watch ESPN? This is the place, but you may have to wait in line. One of the park's few public TVs is inside, and if you're a sports buff, this is the place to be. The scenic patio offers large umbrellas, table service, and a great view of Mother Nature, plus or minus a hundred kids. The lounge also taps a few brews—nothing special, but a mix aimed to please. This is a great place to chill after a long day.

Curry Village, Yosemite Valley. Pizza $8–$20. AE, DC, DISC, MC, V. Summer daily noon–10pm; winter daily noon–9pm. Shuttle-bus stop nos. 13A, 13B, 14, and 20.

Curry Village Taqueria ★ MEXICAN A good place for a quick bite, this taco stand offers rotating daily specials like carne asada and chili verde, along with spicy tacos, burritos, taco salads, beans, and rice.

Curry Village, Yosemite Valley. Most items $3–$10. AE, DC, DISC, MC, V. Mon–Thurs 11am–5pm; Fri–Sun 8am–5pm. Closed in winter. Shuttle-bus stop nos. 13A, 13B, 14, and 20.

Degnan's Cafe AMERICAN Adjacent to Degnan's Deli, this cafe offers specialty coffee drinks, fresh pastries, and ice cream. It's a good place for a quick bite when you're in a hurry—and one of the few spots in the park with Internet kiosks (25¢ per minute).

Yosemite Village, Yosemite Valley. Most items $1–$7. DC, DISC, MC, V. Daily 7am–7pm. Shuttle-bus stop nos. 4 and 10.

Degnan's Deli ★ **Value** DELI A solid delicatessen with a large selection of generous sandwiches made to order (plus incidentals), this is our top choice for a quick, healthy lunch or supper. Sometimes the ordering line gets long, but it moves quickly. This place is half market and half deli; in addition to the made-to-order sandwiches, there is a variety of prepared items—soups, salads, sandwiches, desserts, and snacks—to carry off for a day on the trail. You'll also find a fairly good selection of beer and wine.

Yosemite Village, Yosemite Valley. Most items $3–$8. DC, DISC, MC, V. Daily 7am–7pm. Shuttle-bus stop nos. 4 and 10.

Degnan's Loft (Kids) ITALIAN This cheery restaurant, with a fireplace and beamed ceilings, is adjacent to Degnan's Deli and Degnan's Cafe. It's a good choice for families thanks to the kid-friendly atmosphere. The menu features pizza, pasta, salads, and desserts.

Yosemite Village, Yosemite Valley. Main courses $4.25–$21. DC, DISC, MC, V. Daily noon–9pm. Closed in winter. Shuttle-bus stop nos. 4 and 10.

Mountain Room Restaurant ★★ AMERICAN The best thing about this restaurant is the view. The food's excellent, too, with an emphasis on local organic ingredients, but the floor-to-ceiling windows overlooking Yosemite Falls are simply spectacular—and there's not a bad seat in the house. We suggest the half chicken, which is flavorful and moist, as are the rainbow trout and the Pacific salmon. Meals come complete with vegetables and bread. There are entrees for vegetarians as well as an amazing dessert tray. The Mountain Room also has a good wine list, and the Mountain Room Lounge features an open-air fireplace and an a la carte menu.

Yosemite Lodge at the Falls, Yosemite Valley. www.yosemitepark.com. Main courses $17–$34. AE, DC, DISC, MC, V. Daily 5:30–9pm. Shuttle-bus stop no. 8.

Village Grill AMERICAN The Village Grill is a fast-food joint that's a decent place to pick up a quick bite. It offers burgers, chicken sandwiches, and the like, and has outdoor seating.

Yosemite Village, Yosemite Valley. Most items $5–$10. AE, DC, DISC, MC, V. Daily 11am–5pm. Closed in winter. Shuttle-bus stop no. 2.

Yosemite Lodge Food Court AMERICAN You'll find breakfast, lunch, and dinner at this busy restaurant (serving about 2,000 meals each day), a vast improvement over the traditional cafeteria. It's set up with a series of food stations, where you pick up your choices before heading to the cashier and then to a table either indoors or at the outside seating area, which features tables with umbrellas and good views of Yosemite Falls. The food stations specialize in pasta (with a choice of sauces), pizza, deli sandwiches and salads, a grill (offering burgers, hot dogs, and hot sandwiches), meat-based and vegetarian entrees, desserts and baked goods, and beverages. There's also a hot breakfast station offering traditional American breakfast items and coffee.

Yosemite Lodge at the Falls, Yosemite Valley. Main courses $5–$15. AE, DC, DISC, MC, V. Daily 6:30–10am, 11:30am–2pm, and 5–8:30pm (until 7:30pm in winter). Shuttle-bus stop no. 8.

ELSEWHERE IN THE PARK

Tuolumne Meadows Lodge AMERICAN One of the two restaurants in Yosemite's high country, this lodge offers something for everyone. The breakfast menu features the basics, including eggs, pancakes, fruit, oatmeal, and granola. Dinners always include a beef, chicken, fish, pasta, and vegetarian specialty, all of which change frequently. The mountain trout, citrus salmon pasta, prime rib, and New York steak are consistently good.

Tuolumne Meadows, CA 120. ✆ **209/372-8413.** Reservations required for dinner. Breakfast $7–$11; dinner main courses $6–$28. AE, DC, DISC, MC, V. Daily 7–9am and 6–8pm.

Wawona Dining Room ★★ AMERICAN   The Wawona Hotel's dining room mirrors the hotel's ambience—wide open, lots of windows, sunlight galore. Dinners here are delectable. In addition to some exceptional entrees, such as grilled plum–glazed pork tenderloin skewers with plum compote, rib-eye steak, and several seafood and veggie dishes, there are amazing appetizers like split-pea fritters and crab Louie. Lunch features a variety of sandwiches and salads.

Wawona Hotel, Wawona Rd. ✆ **209/375-1425.** www.yosemitepark.com. Lunch $7–$12; dinner main courses $17–$33. AE, DC, DISC, MC, V. Mon–Sat 11:30am–1:30pm and 5:30–9pm; Sun 10:30am–1:30pm and 5:30–9pm.

White Wolf Lodge AMERICAN   The changing menu in this casual restaurant, with a mountain-lodge atmosphere, offers a variety of standards served up in generous portions. Breakfast choices include eggs, pancakes, omelets, or biscuits and gravy; dinner always features beef, chicken, fish, pasta, and vegetarian dishes. Takeout lunches are also available from noon to 2pm.

White Wolf, Tioga Rd. ✆ **209/372-8416.** Reservations required for dinner. Breakfast $5–$11; dinner main courses $8–$24. AE, DC, DISC, MC, V. Daily 7:30–9:30am and 5–8:30pm.

OUTSIDE THE PARK

To sip a cup of coffee, buy a book, shop for gear, check your e-mail, and relax in a hammock all in one place, visit the **Mountain Sage,** 18653 Main St., Groveland (✆ **209/962-4686;** www.mtnsage.com).

Cafe at the Bug ★★ Value AMERICAN   Ask the Mariposa locals for their favorite place to get a great meal at a reasonable price, and if they'll reveal their secret, it will likely be this bustling eatery. It's a noisy, busy, somewhat self-service restaurant at the Yosemite Bug Rustic Mountain Resort. The casual space contains several rooms with knotty-pine walls, oak floors, wooden chairs and tables, and an open-beamed ceiling. You order at a counter and your food is delivered to your table. The innovative American dishes, with Mediterranean and Californian influences, emphasize organic ingredients, many from an on-site garden. Each night features different offerings: You might have top sirloin, a trout filet with lime butter, or stuffed portobello mushrooms. There is at least one vegetarian and one vegan option at every meal. Breakfasts here range from bacon and eggs to buckwheat pancakes or granola; lunches include sandwiches and sack lunches to go.

At the Yosemite Bug Rustic Mountain Resort & Spa, 6979 CA 140, Midpines. *©* **209/966-6666.** www.yosemitebug.com. Breakfast and lunch items $5–$10; dinner main courses $8–$16. AE, DISC, MC, V. Daily 7am–9pm.

Café Charlotte MEDITERRANEAN   You'll find generous portions of beef, seafood, and pastas in a fine-dining atmosphere at this historic hotel's small dining room. A variety of seasonal specials is offered in addition to staples like charbroiled filet mignon, New York steak, daily seafood entrees, and several vegetarian and vegan choices. Keep an eye out for the delicious artichoke chicken. All meals include veggies, potato or rice, and bread. The wine list is quite good, and there are nightly tastings that feature six local wines for only $5.

At the Hotel Charlotte, 18736 CA 120, Groveland. *©* **209/962-7872.** www.hotel charlotte.com. Reservations recommended. Main courses $10–$23. AE, MC, V. Summer daily 11:30am–4:30pm and 5:30–10pm; fall–spring Thurs–Sun 5:30–9pm.

Castillo's Mexican Food MEXICAN   Established in 1955, this cozy cantina serves heaping portions of well-prepared Mexican favorites. Entrees come with salad, rice, and beans, and can also be ordered a la carte. A house specialty, the *tostada compuesta,* fills a hungry belly with your choice of meat, plus beans, lettuce, and cheese, stuffed into a bowl-shaped crisp tortilla and topped with avocado and sour cream. Various combo plates are available, or you can choose from several steak specialties and seafood dishes such as jumbo shrimp fajitas. For those who like a little extra fire, there's *camarones a la diabla*—shrimp sautéed in butter, garlic, and crushed red chilies. The garden seating is our favorite spot here.

4995 5th St., Mariposa. *©* **209/742-4413.** Reservations recommended in summer. Lunch $6–$13; dinner main courses $8.50–$17. AE, DISC, MC, V. Mon–Thurs 11am–9pm; Fri 11am–9:30pm; Sat 11:30am–9:30pm; Sun 11:30am–2:30pm and 5–8:30pm. Closes 1 hr. earlier in winter.

Cellar Door ★★ NEW AMERICAN   Top-notch food in a rich and refined atmosphere is what you'll experience at this fine restaurant in the landmark Groveland Hotel. The menu has something for everyone and constantly changes to reflect what's fresh and in season. There's a sumptuous local rack of lamb, grilled ahi tuna with wasabi mashers, duck and mushroom risotto, and more. The wine list, which has been lauded by *Wine Spectator,* is fantastic, and the summer season features courtyard dining as well as regularly scheduled concerts under the stars.

At the Groveland Hotel, 18767 CA 120, Groveland. © **800/273-3314** or 209/962-4000. www.groveland.com. Reservations suggested in summer. Lunch $8–$16; dinner main courses $14–$30. AE, DC, DISC, MC, V. Summer Fri–Sun 11am–2pm, daily 6–9pm; winter Tues–Sun 6–8pm.

Charles Street Dinner House ★★ AMERICAN Locally famous for its steaks, the Charles Street Dinner House has been area residents' and visitors' choice for fresh seafood and a variety of other specialties for more than 25 years. We especially recommend the broiled New Zealand rack of lamb with mint glaze; another favorite is the breast of duck with pomegranate glaze. Or try the "scallone"— abalone and scallops sautéed with lemon butter and toasted almonds. The restaurant is located in a historic 1800s building and features decor straight out of the Old West, with a huge wagon wheel in the front window and nice touches such as family photos and fresh flowers. Service is excellent.

5043 Charles St., Mariposa. © **209/966-2366**. www.charlesstreetdinnerhouse.com. Reservations recommended. Main courses $13–$46. AE, DISC, MC, V. Tues–Sat 5–9pm.

Erna's Elderberry House ★★★ EUROPEAN/CALIFORNIAN One of the most renowned eateries in California, this elegant restaurant at Château du Sureau is a feast for the eyes, with a contemporary seating area with purple walls and modern prints adjoining a more traditionally elegant room. Likewise, it is a feast for the taste buds, with a nightly changing menu that will include any number of European culinary traditions sculpted into a meal that is definitively Californian. Offerings might range from marinated mussels and chilled carrot-coconut soup to pan-seared Tasmanian sea trout with oatmeal crust to prosciutto-wrapped beef tenderloin, spinach gnocchi, and blueberry-yogurt terrine. Each menu lists recommended wines to complement the evening's entrees. Proprietor Erna Kubin-Clanin and company also offer regular gourmet cooking classes here.

At Château du Sureau & Spa, 48688 Victoria Lane, Oakhurst. © **559/683-6800**. www.elderberryhouse.com. Reservations recommended. Prix-fixe dinner $95; prix-fixe brunch $44. AE, DISC, MC, V. Daily 5:30–8:30pm; Sun also 11am–1pm.

Happy Burger Diner ★ ⒻFinds AMERICAN One of the best fast-food joints we've seen anywhere, the Happy Burger offers practically any type of fast food you can think of—it has the region's largest menu—with everything cooked fresh to order. The food here takes a few minutes longer than at your usual chain restaurant, but it's worth it. Breakfast (served until 11:30am) includes numerous egg dishes, French toast, pancakes, oatmeal, and the like. The lunch and dinner

menu, available all day, features a multitude of charbroiled burgers, sandwiches, stuffed potatoes, Mexican dishes, salads, and dinner plates such as top sirloin and fried shrimp.

In typical fast-food style, you order your food at the counter; your piping-hot food will then be delivered to your booth, where you'll sit among record album covers from the '60s and '70s and a vintage pinball game.

5120 CA 140 (at 12th St.), Mariposa. © 209/966-2719. www.happyburgerdiner. com. Most items $3–$15. AE, DISC, MC, V. Daily 6am–9pm.

Iron Door Saloon & Grill ★ AMERICAN   In 1852, this family-friendly establishment started serving whiskey from an "'obligatory' plank over two flour barrels," making it California's oldest bar. Now it's the colorful anchor to a city block of businesses (including a soda fountain and a general store), with scads of dollar bills hanging from the ceiling alongside rusted mining equipment, a menagerie of taxidermy, and odd little displays on such topics as the origin of Groveland's name and the career of Black Bart. The menu is fairly basic, listing steaks and burgers and poultry as well as fresh fish and pasta. You can eat in the 150-year-old bar or the adjacent dining room, which is more upscale with tiled floors, rock walls, and historical photographs. Lunch features wraps and salads (plus floats and shakes from the soda fountain). The food and service don't quite live up to the colorful atmosphere, but the Iron Door is a can't-miss nonetheless.

18761 CA 120, Groveland. © 209/962-6244. www.iron-door-saloon.com. Lunch $7–$11; dinner main courses $10–$23. MC, V. Mon–Thurs 11am–9pm; Fri–Sat 11am–10pm. Bar open later.

5

Savoury's ★★ NEW AMERICAN   Open since 2003—with a move to bigger and better quarters in 2009—this is our favorite restaurant in Mariposa. Chef Mirriam Wackerman had catered in the area for years, and customers often urged her to follow her dreams and open a restaurant. Now that she has, the results are extraordinary, with a menu of simple, fresh dishes that meld culinary traditions near and far: jambalaya linguine, chipotle-pesto chicken, spicy shrimp diabla, and hand-cut steaks. For dessert, dig into a decadent panna cotta on a bed of strawberry sauce. The dining room is sleek and stylish, decorated with dried plants and nature photos and art.

5034 CA 140, Mariposa. © 209/966-7677. Main courses $13–$30. AE, DISC, MC, V. Summer daily 5–9:30pm; winter Thurs–Tues 5–9:30pm.

Whoa Nellie Deli ★★ (Finds DELI/INTERNATIONAL FUSION   What looks to be an ordinary gas station is home to a truly extraordinary eatery that serves thousands of people on summer days. Inside the Tioga Gas Mart—aka "The Mobil"—chef Matt "Tioga" Toomey offers some of the most tantalizing plates in the Sierra Nevada, as well as plump to-go sandwiches and pizzas. We recommend you take a seat in a booth or on the popular patio and enjoy the mind-blowing cuisine before moving on. The menu includes fish tacos with mango salsa and ginger slaw, pork tenderloin with apricot-berry glaze, and wild-buffalo meatloaf with garlic mashers. We especially like the lobster taquitos with tomatillo salsa—and the transcendent chocolate cake. All of the plates overflow with excellent salads and heaps of fresh fruit, making the deli the best post-backpacking eatery in the area.

CA 120, just west of U.S. 395, Lee Vining. ℭ **760/647-1088.** Breakfast and lunch $6–$12; dinner main courses $10–$20. MC, V. Daily 7am–9pm. Closed Nov–Apr.

Yosemite Forks Mountain House (Kids) AMERICAN   A reliable stop between Oakhurst and the South Entrance, this family restaurant does a good job with American staples at all three meals a day. For breakfast, options include egg dishes, pancakes, and the like; for lunch, burgers and sandwiches; and for dinner, hearty portions of pasta, steak, and seafood. With exposed beams and log chairs, the atmosphere is appropriately woodsy.

CA 41, at the Bass Lake turnoff, Oakhurst. ℭ **559/683-5191.** Breakfast and lunch $5–$11; dinner main courses $10–$25. DISC, MC, V. Mon–Thurs 7am–9pm; Fri–Sun 6am–9pm.

PICNIC & CAMPING SUPPLIES

If you forget something, chances are you'll be able to get it in the national park's bustling Yosemite Valley, though elsewhere in the park it's tough to find equipment. In the valley, the best place to pick up supplies and camping equipment is the **Yosemite Village Store,** which stocks groceries, film, and maps; it also has an ATM. Nearby, the **Village Sport Shop** carries fishing, camping, and other outdoor gear; plus it sells fishing licenses. The **Yosemite Lodge Gift Shop** and **Curry Village Gift & Grocery** stock some supplies. The **Mountain Shop** in Curry Village sells clothing and equipment for rock climbs, day hikes, and backcountry excursions, while the **Tuolumne Meadows Gift & Mountain Shop** also carries backpacking supplies, including maps and dehydrated food. The **Badger Pass Sport Shop** (open only during the snow season) stocks ski clothing and other winter supplies. There are also several small convenience stores located throughout the park.

In Mariposa, you'll find a good selection of groceries plus a deli at **Pioneer Market,** 5034 Coakley Circle (ℭ **209/742-6100**), behind the town rest area. In Oakhurst, our choice for a grocery store is

Raley's, 40041 CA 41 (© **559/683-8300**). In El Portal, just outside the park's Arch Rock Entrance, you'll find the well-stocked **El Portal Food Market,** on CA 140 (© **209/379-2632**). On the east side of the park in Lee Vining, the upscale **Mono Market** (© **760/647-1010**) can't be beat if you're in search of natural and organic foods.

For better prices, you can stop at the major supermarket and discount chains in **Merced** or **Fresno,** the largest cities in the park's vicinity.

Exploring Sequoia & Kings Canyon

Most of the land in these parks is wilderness, best explored on foot. There are few roads. The three main access points enter the park from the southwest, and much of Sequoia & Kings Canyon remains undeveloped. The National Park Service prefers it that way, as do many visitors. If you visit here after staying in Yosemite, the Grand Canyon, or other big-name national parks, be prepared for a shock. The crowds are thinner, there are few scheduled events, and the prime attraction—and the real reason for the existence of these parks—is the beauty and majesty of the mountains and the trees, some of the largest living things on earth. This is nature, and none of it is likely to change anytime soon. You can expect fewer people, less prepackaged entertainment, and plenty of terrain to explore at your leisure.

1 ESSENTIALS

ACCESS/ENTRY POINTS

You can access the Big Stump Entrance (Kings Canyon National Park) via CA 180, and the Ash Mountain Entrance (Sequoia National Park) via CA 198, both from the west. Continuing east on CA 180 also brings you to an entrance near Cedar Grove Village in the canyon itself, which is open only in summer. See the "Sequoia & Kings Canyon National Parks" map (p. 4) and the "Highway Access to the Parks" map (p. 21) to orient yourself. To access the Mineral King area of Sequoia National Park, take the steep, twisting Mineral King Road (closed in winter) off CA 198, just a few miles outside the Ash Mountain Entrance.

VISITOR CENTERS & INFORMATION

The parks have three major visitor centers open year-round, some seasonal facilities, and a museum. Make one of these facilities your first stop so you can buy books and maps and discuss your plans with park rangers.

(Tips) **Marmot Invasion**

Always do a quick check under your hood before leaving a parking lot. Marmots, especially in the Mineral King area, love munching on car hoses and wiring, leaving a trail of disabled vehicles in their wake. A good number of them have stowed away in a car's engine compartment and hitched rides with unsuspecting drivers to other parts of the parks; several have ridden as far as the Los Angeles area!

In Sequoia National Park, the largest visitor center is **Foothills Visitor Center** (© **559/565-3135**), just inside the Ash Mountain Entrance on CA 198. Exhibits here focus on the Sierra Foothills, a biologically diverse ecosystem.

About 15 miles farther on CA 198 is the **Giant Forest Museum** (© **559/565-4480**), housed in a historic building and offering extensive exhibits on giant sequoias.

Lodgepole Visitor Center (© **559/565-4436**) includes exhibits on geology, wildlife, air quality, and park history. It's located 4½ miles north of Giant Forest Village. Closed weekdays in winter, but it may be open on weekends.

In Kings Canyon National Park, the **Kings Canyon Visitor Center,** in Grant Grove (© **559/565-4307**), includes exhibits on logging and the role of fire in the forests.

Open in summer only are Kings Canyon's small **Cedar Grove Visitor Center** (© **559/565-3793**) and Sequoia's **Mineral King Ranger Station** (© **559/565-3768**), where you can get backcountry permits and information.

FEES

It costs $20 per motor vehicle ($10 per individual on foot, bike, or motorcycle) to enter the park for up to 7 days. Camping fees range from $12 to $20 a night in the park. The Sequoia & Kings Canyon yearly pass, which allows unlimited entry into the park but does not cover camping fees, sells for $30. Also see "Special Permits & Passes," in chapter 2.

REGULATIONS

In Sequoia & Kings Canyon, there is a 14-day camping limit from June 14 to September 14, with a maximum of 30 camping days per year. Check campsite bulletin boards for additional regulations. Some campgrounds close in winter (see the chart on p. 134). Pets are

allowed in campgrounds, but they must be on a leash and are not
allowed on any trails.

The most important warning in Sequoia & Kings Canyon, which cannot be repeated too often, is that this is **bear country,** and proper food storage is required for the safety and health of both visitors and the resident black bears. In addition, rattlesnakes are common, so be careful where you put your feet and hands. In the Foothills area, check your clothes frequently for ticks; poison oak is another hazard.

The roads in the park are particularly steep and winding. Those in RVs will find it easiest to come by way of CA 180 from Fresno.

---

2 ORIENTATION

The parks are roughly equidistant—5 hours by car—from both San Francisco and Los Angeles. Kings Canyon National Park borders Sequoia National Park on the north and is nearest to Yosemite and Fresno. Kings Canyon contains the developed areas of Grant Grove and Cedar Grove. Sequoia National Park is home to the Giant Forest sequoia grove, as well as Lodgepole, the Foothills, and Mineral King. The main entrance (for all except Mineral King) is on CA 198, via Ash Mountain through Visalia and Three Rivers. From Sequoia's border, Visalia is 36 miles and Three Rivers is 7 miles away.

Although it's impossible to drive through the parks from west to east—the High Sierras get in the way—a north-south road, the Generals Highway, connects Grant Grove in Kings Canyon National Park with Giant Forest in Sequoia National Park. The highway runs 25 miles between two giant sequoias named for famous American generals—the General Grant Tree and the General Sherman Tree. Allow at least an hour to drive between the two on this slow, winding route—not including delays for construction, planned for the foreseeable future. From several miles inside the CA 198 Ash Mountain Entrance to Giant Forest, the Generals Highway is narrow and winding and not recommended for vehicles over 22 feet long, which should enter the parks from CA 180.

The road to Mineral King turns south off CA 198 about 3 miles east of Three Rivers, crosses private and public land, and heads 11 miles to the Lookout Point Entrance. From here it's another 15 miles to Mineral King. This steep, narrow, twisting dead-end road is closed in winter and does not reconnect with any other park roadways, which puts the Mineral King area off-limits to motor vehicles during the winter and well into spring.

INTRODUCING SEQUOIA NATIONAL PARK

The best-known stand of sequoias in the world can be found in **Giant Forest,** part of Sequoia National Park. Named in 1875 by explorer and environmentalist John Muir, this area consists mostly of huge meadows and a large grove of trees. At the northern edge of the grove, you can't miss the **General Sherman Tree,** considered the largest living tree on the planet, although it is neither the tallest nor the widest. Its size is noteworthy because of the tree's mass—experts estimate the weight of its trunk at about 1,385 tons. The General Sherman Tree is 275 feet tall, it measures 102½ feet around at its base, and its largest branch is 6¾ feet in diameter. It is believed to be about 2,100 years old—*and it's still growing.* Every year, it adds enough new wood to make another 60-foot-tall tree. The tree is part of the 2-mile **Congress Trail,** a foot trail that includes groups of trees with names such as the Senate and the House. Also in the area is the **Beetle Rock Education Center,** a fun place for kids to investigate science and nature.

Another interesting stop in Giant Forest is **Tharp's Log,** a cabin named after the first non–Native American settler in the area, Hale Tharp, who grazed cattle among the giant sequoias and built a summer cabin in the 1860s from a fallen sequoia hollowed by fire. It is the oldest cabin remaining in the park.

Pretty **Crescent Meadow** is a pristine clearing dotted with wildflowers and tall grasses. A trail (described in "The Highlights" section below) wraps around the meadow. This is also the trail head for several backcountry hikes.

Also in the area is **Moro Rock,** a large granite dome well worth the half-hour climb up and back. From the top, Moro Rock offers one of the most spectacular views of the dark and barren Great Western

---

Fun Facts   A Question of Size

Until recently, the National Park Service has claimed that the General Sherman Tree is the largest living thing on earth. Technically, however, this may not be quite true, and now the claim is that it's the largest living tree, still quite a distinction. The reason for the change? Park officials say it has been discovered that some underground fungi may actually be bigger than the General Sherman Tree. In addition, there are groves of aspen trees in the Rockies that share a common root system and may be considered one living thing, thereby exceeding the General in overall size.

Halstead Meadow

Generals Highway

Wuksachi Village 7200 ft.

Lodgepole Visitor Center

Lodgepole Village 6720 ft.

← To Grant Grove

Marble Fork Kaweah River

Generals Highway

Wolverton

Wolverton Pack Station

General Sherman Tree

General Lee Tree

Giant Forest Museum

Beetle Rock Education Center

Tharp's Log

Crescent Meadow Rd. (closed in winter)

Crescent Meadow

To Ash Mountain Entrance

Auto Log

Tunnel Log

Moro Rock 6725 ft.

KINGS CANYON NATIONAL PARK

Area of Detail

SEQUOIA NATIONAL PARK

Campground

Picnic Area

Ranger Station

0   10 mi

0   10 km

Divide, which includes the Kaweah Range. The divide is one of two crests in the southern Sierra Nevada, but is not officially the main crest, which lies to the east and is obscured from view.

Lodgepole Village, the most developed area in both parks, lies just northeast of Giant Forest on the Generals Highway. Here you'll find the largest visitor center in the parks, plus a large market, several places to eat, a laundry, a post office, and showers.

Nearby, the **Wuksachi Village** has replaced the old facilities that were damaging to the Giant Forest sequoia grove. A dining room, gift shop, and lodge have all recently opened.

About 16 miles south of Giant Forest are the **Foothills.** Located near the Ash Mountain Entrance, the Foothills area offers a visitor center, several campgrounds, a picnic area, and **Hospital Rock,** a large boulder with ancient pictographs believed to have been painted by the Monache Indians who once lived here. Nearby are about 50 grinding spots probably used to smash acorns into flour. A short trail leads down to a serene place along the Kaweah River where the water gushes over rapids into deep, clear pools.

6

Located in the southern part of the park, **Mineral King** is a pristine high-mountain valley carved by glaciers and bordered by the tall peaks of the Great Western Divide. Red and orange shales mix with white marble, black metamorphic shale, and granite to give the rocky landscape a rainbow of hues. This area resembles the Rocky Mountains more than the rest of the Sierra Nevada because the peaks are formed of metamorphic rock. A silver prospector gave Mineral King its name in the 1800s, and the region was annexed to the park in 1978. The trails in Mineral King begin at 7,500 feet and climb. To reach the area, head west from the Ash Mountain Entrance 3 miles on CA 198 to the turnoff—watch for the sign. Then it's a 28-mile trip that makes around 700 tight turns and takes 1½ hours. Trailers, RVs, and buses are not allowed. The road is closed in winter, when the area is prone to avalanches.

INTRODUCING KINGS CANYON NATIONAL PARK

With its rugged canyon, huge river, and desolate backcountry, Kings Canyon is considered a hiker's dream. Kings Canyon comprises Grant Grove and Cedar Grove, as well as portions of the Monarch Wilderness and Jennie Lakes Wilderness. *Note:* Between Grant Grove and Cedar Grove is Giant Sequoia National Monument, which is managed as part of Sequoia National Forest. This region includes Hume Lake, Boyden Cavern, and several campgrounds.

Grant Grove is the most crowded region in either national park. Here you'll find the towering **General Grant Tree** amid a grove of spectacular giant sequoias. The tree was discovered by Joseph Hardin Tomas in 1862, and named 5 years later by Lucretia P. Baker to honor Ulysses S. Grant. The tree measures 267½ feet tall and 107½ feet around, and is thought to be the world's third-largest living tree, possibly 2,000 years old (just a youngster in this neighborhood!). It was officially declared the "Nation's Christmas Tree" by President Calvin Coolidge in 1926, and remains the centerpiece of an annual Christmas tree ceremony.

Two and a half miles southwest of the grove is the **Big Stump Trail,** an instructive hike that can be slightly depressing as it winds among the remains of logged sequoias. Since sequoia wood decays slowly, you'll see century-old piles of leftover sawdust that remain from the logging days. In summer, visitors can drive a short distance to **Panoramic Point,** stand atop this 7,520-foot ledge, and look across a long stretch of the Sierra Nevada for a glimpse of Kings Canyon.

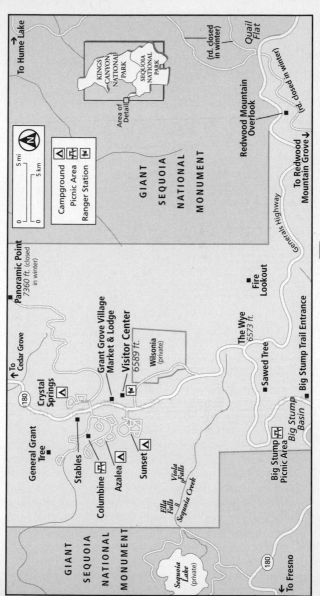

To Hume Lake

Panoramic Point
7360 ft. (closed
in winter)

To
Cedar Grove

Crystal
Springs

General Grant
Tree

Stables

Columbine

Azalea

Sunset

Ella
Falls

Viola
Falls

Sequoia Creek

Sequoia Lake
(private)

To Fresno

180

180

GIANT
SEQUOIA
NATIONAL
MONUMENT

Grant Grove Village
Market & Lodge

Visitor Center
6589 ft.

Wilsonia
(private)

The Wye
6573 ft.

Fire
Lookout

Sawed Tree

Big Stump
Basin

Big Stump
Picnic Area

Big Stump Trail Entrance

Generals Highway

To Redwood
Mountain Grove

(rd. closed
in winter)

Redwood Mountain
Overlook

Quail
Flat

GIANT
SEQUOIA
NATIONAL
MONUMENT

KINGS
CANYON
NATIONAL
PARK

SEQUOIA
NATIONAL
PARK

Area of
Detail

Campground
Picnic Area
Ranger Station

0   5 mi
0   5 km

N

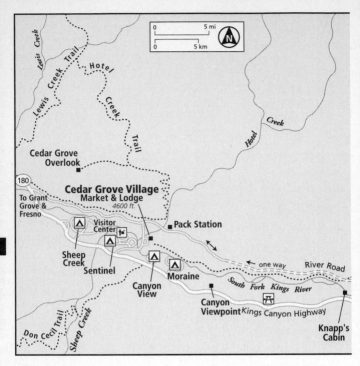

Although in the same park, **Cedar Grove** seems a world away. That this region is even around today is sheer luck. There were once plans to flood Kings Canyon by damming the Kings River, a decision that would have buried Cedar Grove beneath a deep lake. Today, that's considered an inconceivable move. With the flood threat abated, the region stood to become another Yosemite, but people fought hard to avoid the overcrowding and development that had occurred in Yosemite, and eventually everyone agreed it was better to keep development to a minimum. It was finally annexed in 1965 and, under a master plan for the area, will remain as it is today.

Cedar Grove is abundant with lush foliage, crashing waterfalls, and miles upon miles of solitude. Half the fun of driving through Kings Canyon is seeing its sheer granite walls close around you and the wild South Fork of the Kings River tumble by. The small **Cedar Grove Village** contains a store and gift shop, restaurant, laundry, showers, lodge, and campgrounds. This region of the park is often less crowded

Campground ▲
Picnic Area ⌷
Hiking Trail ·······
Ranger Station ⌷

KINGS CANYON NATIONAL PARK

Area of Detail

SEQUOIA NATIONAL PARK

Copper Creek Trail

Granite Creek

■ **North Dome**
8717 ft.

Wilderness Permit Station (Road's End)

Grand Sentinel Viewpoint

To Mist Falls

Motor Nature Trail

KINGS CANYON

River Trail

Zumwalt Meadow Trail

Muir Rock

Grand Sentinel
8540 ft.

KINGS

Roaring River

Roaring River Falls

than others. Remember that it is also closed from mid-November to mid-April.

One mile east of the Cedar Grove Village turnoff is **Canyon View,** where visitors can see the glacially carved U-shape of Kings Canyon.

Easily accessible nature trails in Cedar Grove include Zumwalt Meadow, Roaring River Falls, and Knapp's Cabin. **Zumwalt Meadow** is dotted with ponderosa pine and has good views of two rock formations: **Grand Sentinel** and **North Dome.** The top of Grand Sentinel is 8,504 feet above sea level, while North Dome, which some say resembles Half Dome in Yosemite, tops out at 8,717 feet. The mile-long trail around the meadow is one of the prettiest in the park. The best place to access this walk is at a parking lot 4½ miles east of the turnoff for Cedar Grove Village.

Roaring River Falls is a 5-minute walk from the parking area, 3 miles east of the turnoff to Cedar Grove Village. Even during summers and dry years, the water here crashes through a narrow granite

A Nearby National Monument

Some of the most beautiful scenery in the Sequoia & Kings Canyon National Parks area is not actually in either of these national parks, but in an adjacent section of the Sequoia National Forest that was recently designated a national monument.

Covering 328,000 acres, **Giant Sequoia National Monument** was created by President Bill Clinton in 2000. The monument contains 38 groves of sequoias, including some of the most magnificent giant trees to be seen anywhere. In addition, it has towering domes of granite; scenic **Hume Lake,** a popular destination for boaters and anglers; and the spectacular **Kings Canyon**—the deepest canyon in North America, with elevations ranging from 1,000 to 11,000 feet.

Among the hiking trails in the monument is the **Boole Tree Trail,** a moderate 2.5-mile loop trail that leads to Boole Tree, the largest sequoia in the 1.1-million-acre Sequoia National Forest, and the eighth-largest tree in the world. This trail, located off Forest Road 13S55, off Kings Canyon Highway, includes forest and open country, where you'll see

chute into a cold green pool below. During a wet spring, these falls are powerful enough to drench visitors who venture too close. **Knapp's Cabin** can be reached via a short walk from a turnoff 2 miles east of the road to Cedar Grove Village. Here, during the 1920s, Santa Barbara businessman George Knapp commissioned lavish fishing expeditions and used this tiny cabin to store his expensive gear.

The **Monarch Wilderness** is a 45,000-acre region protected under the 1984 California Wilderness Act. Part of it lies on the grounds of Sequoia National Forest, adjoining the wilderness in Kings Canyon National Park. It's tough to reach, and so steep that hikers practically need to be roped in to climb. You're close to the wilderness area when you pass Kings Canyon Lodge and Boyden Cavern.

The **Jennie Lakes Wilderness** is even smaller at 10,500 acres. Although tiny enough to hike through in a day, it exhibits a variety of wilderness features, including the 10,365-foot Mitchell Peak and several wide lowland meadows. This region lies between the Generals Highway and CA 180, east of Grant Grove. About 7 miles southeast of Grant Grove, Big Meadows Road (closed in winter) takes off from sequoias, scenic vistas of the Kings River, and wildflowers in summer.

An easy walk on the quarter-mile (one-way) **Chicago Stump Trail** leads to the stump of the General Noble Tree, which was cut down, chopped into pieces, and then reassembled and displayed at the 1893 World's Fair in Chicago. Some fairgoers refused to believe that a tree could grow so big and dubbed it "the California hoax."

Information about other attractions and facilities within the monument, such as the beautiful drive through Kings Canyon and the underground world of Boyden Cavern, are discussed elsewhere in this book.

Primitive camping is allowed and there is no fee. For additional information on Giant Sequoia National Monument, contact the **Hume Lake Ranger District,** Sequoia National Forest, 35860 E. Kings Canyon Rd. (CA 180), Dunlap, CA 93621 (© **559/338-2251;** www.r5.fs.fed.us/sequoia).

Generals Highway and heads east into Sequoia National Forest. From this road you can access several trails that lead into Jennie Lakes Wilderness.

3 THE HIGHLIGHTS

The view atop **Moro Rock** is one of the most spectacular in the Sierra—the Great Western Divide dominates the eastern horizon. These high-elevation barren mountains can seem dark and ominous, even though snow caps the ridgeline throughout the year. The cliffs appear towering and steep, and with some peaks over 13,000 feet, they are only slightly below the summit of Mount Whitney (14,474 ft.), which is obscured from view. The climb to the top of the Rock takes you up hundreds of stairs, so pace yourself. The summit offers a narrow, fenced plateau with endless views. During a full moon, the mountain peaks shimmer like silver. See "Seeing the Parks by Car," below.

Mist Falls is a wide, powerful waterfall accessible only on foot (see chapter 7), but the trek is well worth the effort. The waterfall is especially impressive during spring and early summer, when it's fed by snowmelt, and the cascading water crashing onto the rocks below drowns out most other sounds. This is also when you're likely to see rainbows galore.

Crescent Meadow is a large, picturesque clearing dotted with high grass and wildflowers, and encircled by a forest of firs and sequoias. The park's oldest cabin is along this route as well. This is a particularly nice hike in early morning and at dusk, when the indirect sunlight allows for the best photography (see chapter 7).

4 EXPLORE THE INSIDE OF THE EARTH IN TWO CAVES

Although there are more than 200 caves in this area, only two are open for tours by the general public—one in Sequoia National Park and the other in Giant Sequoia National Monument, just outside Kings Canyon National Park.

South of the Giant Forest in Sequoia National Park is the turnoff from CA 198 for **Crystal Cave,** a beautiful underground world that was formed from limestone that turned to marble. The cave contains an array of cave formations, many still growing, that range from sharply pointed stalactites and towering stalagmites to elaborate flowing draperies. To reach the entrance, drive 7 miles down the narrow winding road (RVs, trailers, and buses are prohibited), and walk 0.5 miles down a steep path to the cave. *Note:* To take a tour, you need to get advance tickets, available at both the Lodgepole and the Foothills visitor centers. Tickets are not sold at the cave.

The Sequoia Natural History Association conducts 45-minute **guided tours** along paved, lighted pathways. The tours are offered from mid-June to Labor Day, daily every half-hour from 10:30am to 4:30pm; from mid-May to mid-June and after Labor Day to late September, daily every hour from 11am to 3pm (with slightly longer weekend hours). The cost is $11 for adults, $10 for seniors 62 and

Impressions

It is in this cave [Crystal Cave] that nature has lavishly traced her design in decorative glory.

—Park Superintendent Walter Fry, 1925

special **discovery tour** is offered in summer only, Monday through Friday at 4:15pm. It is less structured and limited to 16 people, has a minimum age requirement of 13, and costs $19 per person. The cave is a constant 48°F (9°C), so take a sweater or jacket. Sturdy footwear is recommended, and strollers, tripods, and backpacks are prohibited. Information is available at visitor centers or by telephone (© **559/ 565-3759**).

Ten miles west of Cedar Grove, in Giant Sequoia National Monument, is **Boyden Cavern,** the only other cave in the area that hosts tours. Boyden is an especially scenic cave, known for a wide variety of formations including rare "shields," which consist of two roughly circular halves that look like flattened clam shells. Highlights include a flowstone formation, known as Mother Nature's Wedding Cake, and the appropriately named Christmas Tree and Baby Elephant formations. The cave is open daily from late April through mid-November. Hours are usually 10am to 5pm in June, but often are shorter at the beginning and end of the season. Visitors get to see the cave on guided 45-minute tours that follow a well-lighted, handrail-equipped trail. Tours leave approximately every hour on the hour. The cost is $13 for ages 13 and up, $8 for children 3 to 12; admission is free for children 2 and younger. Reservations are not required. Special flashlight tours (bring your own flashlight) are also available, by reservation only, Friday and Saturday evenings, at the same prices as the regular tours. For information, contact **Boyden Cavern Adventures** (© **559/338-0959;** www.caverntours.com).

5 HOW TO SEE THE PARKS IN 1 OR 2 DAYS

Eighty percent of the parks' visitors come here on day trips—an amazing statistic considering the geography of this place. It takes 3 to 4 days to do the parks justice, but it is possible to take a short walk through a grove of big trees in an afternoon. Day-trippers should stick to Grant Grove, if possible—it's the most accessible. Coming from the south, Giant Forest is a good alternative, although the trip takes a while on the steep and narrow Generals Highway. Cedar Grove and Mineral King, two other destination points, are farther afield and require an early start or an overnight stay.

If you have only 1 day, we recommend driving from the Foothills through Giant Forest to Grant Grove, or vice versa. It's about 2 hours through the park, plus whatever additional time is necessary to

> **Tips** **A Vacation from Your Car**
>
> Since 2007, the National Park Service and the City of Visalia
> have operated a transportation system that makes it possible
> to explore Sequoia National Park without a car. From Visalia
> (or Three Rivers), the **Sequoia Shuttle** (© **877/287-4453;**
> www.sequoiashuttle.com) will take you to the Giant Forest
> Museum for just $15 round-trip. From here, riders can connect
> with the **free park shuttle** to get to Wuksachi Lodge or one of
> the numerous trail heads en route. The former makes five runs
> between 7am and 6:30pm daily (reservations are accepted);
> the latter runs from 9am to 6pm daily. Both shuttles operate
> in the summer only.

resume your route outside its entrances. Start at a park visitor center—there's one near each location—to get your bearings. Whether traveling from the north or south, you'll see the varied terrain within the park as you pass through dense forest, exposed meadows, and scrubby foothills covered in oaks and underbrush. In spring and summer, much of the route may be dotted with wildflowers. The southern portion runs along the Kaweah River. This route also passes two large stands of giant sequoias: one at Grant Grove and the other at Giant Forest. Both have easy trails looping through the majestic stands. At Grant Grove, a footpath passes lengthwise through a fallen sequoia.

6 SEEING THE PARKS BY CAR

Although these two parks are generally considered the domain of hikers, and they contain only 127 miles of paved roads between them, you will have a use for your car here. Those not willing or physically able to lace up a pair of hiking boots and take off down a trail will still be able to enjoy the scenery, often from the comfort of their motor vehicle or from roadside and near-roadside viewpoints.

The **Generals Highway** runs nearly 50 miles from Sequoia National Park's Ash Mountain Entrance to Grant Grove in Kings Canyon National Park, passing through the Giant Forest, home of the world's largest sequoia trees. It's a very pretty drive, with optional stops to see the Giant Forest Museum and the General Sherman Tree. There are also several easy walking trails along the way (see chapter 7 for details). From several miles inside the Ash Mountain Entrance to

Giant Forest, Generals Highway is narrow and winding and not recommended for vehicles over 22 feet long.

For a short, scenic drive in Sequoia National Park, we recommend the paved **Moro Rock/Crescent Meadow Road,** a 3-mile dead-end road (open in summer only) that runs from the Giant Forest Museum, along the Generals Highway, south and east through a grove of sequoias. Along the way, you can see the fallen sequoia at Auto Log (now too rotted to support a vehicle), drive through a hollowed-out fallen sequoia at Tunnel Log, and stop for a steep 0.3-mile walk up to the top of Moro Rock for a spectacular panoramic view. This road ends at Crescent Meadow, known for its colorful wildflowers in summer. See also the sections on Moro Rock and Crescent Meadow in "The Highlights," above.

Kings Canyon Highway, from the Grant Grove area to Cedar Grove in Kings Canyon National Park, is a lovely drive of some 35 miles, but most of its especially scenic sections are not in the park. Instead, some of the best roadside scenery is in Giant Sequoia National Monument (see "A Nearby National Monument," above). For part of the journey, Kings Canyon Highway (also called CA 180) is high above the Kings River, offering breathtaking vistas of the canyon; then it seems to almost join the river, giving motorists a close-up view of the rapids as the water crashes over and among huge boulders. Well worth a stop along this route are the spectacular Grizzly Falls. Allow about an hour. The eastern two-thirds of this road are open during the summer only.

Hikes & Other Outdoor Pursuits in Sequoia & Kings Canyon

1 DAY HIKES & SCENIC WALKS

Sequoia & Kings Canyon are an absolute paradise for hikers. This is not only because the parks have a huge network of trails—some 800 miles' worth—but also because of the vast and relatively untouched wilderness here. In fact, over 85% of the parks' land—some 736,980 acres—is designated wilderness, accessible only to those on foot or horseback. But it's wrong to assume that this means the parks are only for the hard-core backpacker. In fact, you can see quite a bit of the parks on a number of short walks and day hikes. In many cases, after just 5 minutes on the trail, you'll feel you've left the civilized world behind. At almost any point that you choose to venture away from the highway, you're likely to find an abundance of natural wonders: colorful flora, interesting fauna, and beautiful landscape created over millions of years of solitude. Below, we suggest day hikes that will help you experience the best these parks have to offer. A trail map can be very helpful; some trail intersections are confusing, and signs can disappear.

Big Trees Trail and the trail to General Sherman Tree are wheelchair accessible, but several paved trails in the Giant Forest area can also be negotiated by wheelchair, depending on individual ability. See www.nps.gov/seki/planyourvisit/accessibility.htm for additional information.

NEAR GIANT FOREST

Big Trees Trail This scenic loop walk among the sequoias skirts a pretty meadow, with trailside exhibits that explain why this area is such a good habitat for sequoias. There are usually abundant wildflowers in Round Meadow in early summer. The trail is wheelchair accessible, paved with some wooden boardwalk sections.

0.7 miles/1 hr. Easy. Start at the Giant Forest Museum.

Congress Trail ★ This self-guided walk circles some of Sequoia National Park's most well-known and best-loved giants. The trail is a paved loop with a 200-foot elevation gain. Here you'll find the General Sherman Tree, considered to be the largest living tree on earth. The Lincoln Tree is nearby, along with several clusters of trees including the House and the Senate. Try standing in the middle of these small groups of trees to gain the perspective of an ant at a picnic. The walk is also dotted with inviting benches.

2 miles/1–3 hr. Easy. Start at the General Sherman Tree, just off the Generals Hwy., 2 miles northeast of Giant Forest Museum.

Crescent Meadow Loop ★ The meadow is a large, picturesque clearing dotted with high grass and wildflowers, encircled by a forest of firs and sequoias. The park's oldest cabin (Tharp's Log) is along this paved route as well. This is a particularly nice hike in early morning and at dusk, when the indirect sunlight provides the best photo opportunities.

1.8 miles/1–3 hr. Easy. Begin at the Crescent Meadow parking area.

Hazelwood Nature Trail   Follow the signs for a good walk that winds among several stands of sequoias, accompanied by exhibits that explain the relationship among trees, fire, and humans.

1 mile/1 hr. Easy. Begin on the south side of the Generals Hwy., across from the road to Round Meadow.

High Sierra Trail ★★   This is one gateway to the backcountry, but the first few miles of the trail also make a great day hike. Along the way, you'll find spectacular views of the Kaweah River's Middle Fork and the Great Western Divide. The trail runs along a south-facing slope, so it's warm in spring and fall. Get an early start in summer. From the trail head, cross two wooden bridges over Crescent Creek until you reach a junction. Tharp's Log is to the left, with the High Sierra Trail to the right. Hike uphill through the damage done by the Buckeye Fire of 1988, a blaze ignited by a discarded cigarette 3,000 feet below, near the Kaweah River. After hiking 0.8 miles, you'll reach Eagle View, which offers a picturesque vision of the Great Western Divide. On the south side of the canyon are the craggy Castle Rocks. Continue on to see Panther Rock, Alta Peak, and Alta Meadow. At 2.8 miles is a sign for the Wolverton Cutoff, a trail used as a stock route between the Wolverton trail head and the high country. A bit farther on, you'll come upon Panther Creek and a small waterfall. At 3.3 miles, you'll see pink-and-gray Panther Rock. Follow a few more creeks to reach the last fork of Panther Creek, running down a steep, eroded ravine.

9 miles/6 hr. Moderate. The trail head is near the restrooms at the Crescent Meadow parking area.

Huckleberry Trail ★★   This is a great hike, offering tremendous beauty without the crush of too many people. It passes through forests and meadows, near a 100-year-old cabin, and by an old American Indian village. The first mile of this hike takes you along the Hazelwood Nature Trail (see above). Head south at each junction until you see a big sign with blue lettering that marks the start of the Huckleberry Trail. You'll pass a small creek and meadow before reaching a second sign to Huckleberry Meadow. The next mile is steep and crosses beneath sequoias, dogwoods, and white firs. At the 1.5-mile point is Squatter's Cabin, a log building built in the 1880s. East of the cabin is a trail junction. Head north (left) up a short hill. At the next junction, veer left along the edges of Circle Meadow for about 0.3

detour to Bear's Bathtub, a pair of sequoias hollowed by fire and filled with water. Legend has it that an old mountain guide named Chester Wright once surprised a bear taking a bath here, hence its name. Continue on the trail heading northeast to the Washington Tree, which is almost as big as the General Sherman Tree, and then on to Alta Trail. Turn west (left) to Little Deer Creek. On both sides of the creek are American Indian mortar holes. At the next junction, head north (right) to return to the Generals Highway and the last leg of the Huckleberry Trail to the parking area.

4 miles/2–3 hr. Moderate. Begin at the Hazelwood Nature Trail parking area, $\frac{1}{3}$ mile east of Giant Forest Museum on the Generals Hwy.

Moro Rock ★★
This walk climbs 300 feet up 400 steps that twist along this gigantic boulder perched perilously on a ridge top. Take it slowly. The view from the top is breathtaking, stretching to the Great Western Divide, which looks barren and dark, like the end of the world. The mountains are often snowcapped well into summer. During a full moon, the view is even stranger and more beautiful.

0.3 miles/30 min.–1 hr. Moderate. Begin at the Moro Rock parking area.

Moro Rock & Soldiers Loop Trail
This hike cuts cross-country from the Giant Forest Village to Moro Rock, heading through a forest dotted with giant sequoias. Be advised that a carpet of ferns occasionally hides the trail. It pops out at Moro Rock, and then it's just a quick heart-thumper to the top (see the trail description above).

4.6 miles/3–4 hr. Moderate. The trail head is just west of Giant Forest Museum.

Trail of the Sequoias
This trail offers a longer, more remote hike into Giant Forest, away from the crowds and along some of the more scenic points of the plateau. The first 0.3 miles is along the Congress Trail before heading uphill at Alta Trail. Look for signs that read TRAIL OF THE SEQUOIAS. After 1.5 miles, including a 0.5-mile steep climb among giant sequoias, you'll encounter the ridge of the Giant Forest. Here you'll find a variety of trees, young and old, fallen and sturdy. Notice the shallow root system of fallen trees and the lightning-blasted tops of others still standing. The trail continues to Log Meadow, past Crescent Meadow, and to Chimney Tree, a sequoia hollowed by fire. At the junction with Huckleberry Trail, follow the blue and green signs straight (north) toward Sherman Tree and back to Congress Trail.

6 miles/4 hr. Moderate. The trail head is at the northeast end of the General Sherman Tree parking area.

Azalea Trail This is a pleasant trail at any time, and particularly beautiful in late June and early July when the azaleas along Sequoia Creek are in full, fragrant bloom. From the visitor center, walk past the amphitheater to the Sunset Campground and cross CA 180. The first mile joins the South Boundary Trail as it meanders through Wilsonia and crisscrosses Sequoia Creek in a gentle climb. After 1.5 miles, you'll come to the third crossing of Sequoia Creek, which may be dry in late summer, but still lush with ferns and brightly colored azaleas along its banks. Return the way you came.

3 miles/1–2 hr. Easy. The trail head begins at the Kings Canyon Visitor Center.

Big Stump Trail This trail meanders through what was once a grove of giant sequoias. All that's left today are the old stumps and piles of 100-year-old sawdust. A brochure available at the visitor centers describes the logging that occurred here in the 1880s. To continue onward, see the Hitchcock Meadow Trail described below, which leads to Viola Fall.

1 mile/1 hr. Easy. Begin at the Big Stump Picnic Area near the CA 180 entrance to Grant Grove from Kings Canyon.

Dead Giant Loop This easy, meandering loop trail takes you along a lush meadow to the shell of what was once an impressive forest giant. The Dead Giant Loop and the North Grove Loop (described below) share the first 0.8 miles. The trail descends a fire road and, after 0.3 miles, hits a junction. Take the lower trail, continuing along the fire road. After another 0.5 miles, you'll break off from the North Grove Loop and head south around a lush meadow. It's another 0.3 miles to a sign that reads DEAD GIANT. Turn right (west) to see what's left of this large sequoia. The trail climbs slightly as it circles a knoll and comes to Sequoia Lake Overlook. The lake was formed in 1899 when the Kings River Lumber Company built a dam on Mill Flat Creek. The water was diverted down a flume to the town of Sanger. During logging times, millions of board feet of giant sequoias were floated down that flume to be finished at a mill in Sanger. Continue around the loop back to the DEAD GIANT sign and then head back to the parking area.

2.3 miles/1½ hr. Easy. The trail head is at the lower end of the General Grant Tree parking area. It begins near a locked gate with a sign that reads NORTH GROVE LOOP.

General Grant Tree Trail (Kids) This walk leads to the huge General Grant Tree, which is the nation's only living national shrine. In 1956, U.S. President Eisenhower gave the Grant Tree this designation in memory of Americans who gave their lives in wartime. The walk includes signs to help visitors interpret forest features.

0.6 miles/30 min. Easy. Begin at the Grant Tree parking area 1 mile northwest of the visitor center.

Hitchcock Meadow Trail   This trail leads to the pretty Viola Fall. The first 0.5 miles mirrors the Big Stump Trail described above. From here, hike another 0.3 miles to the Hitchcock sequoia stumps. Notice the small sequoias in this area; they are descendants of the giant sequoias logged in the last century. At this point, the trail climbs slightly to a ridge, where it reenters Kings Canyon National Park before descending steeply to Sequoia Creek. Cross the creek on a culvert bridge toward a sign directing hikers to Viola Fall, a series of short steps that, during high water, merge into a single fall. It's dangerous to venture down into the canyon, but above it are several flat places that make great picnic spots.

3.5 miles/2 hr. Easy. Begin at the Big Stump Picnic Area near the entrance to Grant Grove from Kings Canyon.

North Grove Loop   This trail follows an abandoned mill road from yesteryear. It cuts through stands of dogwood, sugar pine, sequoia, and white fir. You'll find a large, dead sequoia that shows evidence of a fire.

1.5 miles/1–2 hr. Easy. Begin at the lower end of the General Grant Tree parking area.

Park Ridge Trail   Begin by walking south along the ridge, where views of the valley and peaks dominate. On a clear day, you can see Hume Lake in Sequoia National Forest, the San Joaquin Valley, and occasionally the Coast Range 100 miles away. Return the way you came.

4.7 miles/3 hr. Easy. Begin at the Panoramic Point parking area, a 2.5-mile drive down a steep road from Grant Grove Village.

Sunset Trail   This hike climbs 1,400 feet past two waterfalls and a lake. After crossing the highway, the trail moves to the left around a campground. After 1.3 miles, you'll follow the South Boundary Trail toward Viola Fall. You'll then reach a paved road where you can head to the right to see the park's original entrance. Return the way you came, or follow the road to the General Grant Tree parking area and walk to the visitor center.

6 miles/3–4 hr. Moderate to strenuous. Begin across the road from the Kings Canyon Visitor Center.

NEAR CEDAR GROVE
Bubbs Creek Trail ★   The Bubbs Creek Trail begins by crossing and recrossing Copper Creek. This site was once an American Indian

Impressions

We are gathered here around a tree that is worthy of represent-
ing the spirit of America on Christmas Day. That spirit is best
expressed in the plain things of life, the love of the family circle,
the simple life of the out-of-doors. The tree is a pillar that is a tes-
timony that things of the spirit transcend those of the flesh.
—Colonel John White, former Sequoia & Kings Canyon
National Parks superintendent, at a National Christmas Tree
ceremony

village, and shards of obsidian can still be found on the ground. After
the first mile, you'll enter a swampy area that offers a good place to
watch for wildlife. The trail here closes in on the river, where deer and
bears drink. At 2 miles, you'll come to a junction. The trail to Paradise
Valley heads north (left), while the hike to Bubbs Creek veers right
and crosses Bailey Bridge, over the South Fork of the Kings River.
Continue east over the four small wooden bridges that cross Bubbs
Creek. The creek was named after John Bubbs, a prospector and
rancher who arrived here in 1864. The trail will climb on the creek's
north side, throwing in a few steep switchbacks to keep you alert. The
switchbacks provide nice alternating views of the canyon of Paradise
Valley and Cedar Grove. At 3 miles, you'll come to a large emerald
pool with waterfalls. Far above is a rock formation known as the
Sphinx—John Muir named the feature after Egypt's famous likeness.
At 4 miles, you'll reach Sphinx Creek, a nice place to spend the day
or night (with a wilderness permit). There are several campsites
nearby. Hike back the way you came or on the Sentinel Trail.

8 miles/5 hr. Moderate to strenuous. The trail head is at the east end of the parking
area at Road's End.

Mist Falls ★★ This is one of the more popular trails leading to
the backcountry, but it also makes a nice day hike. The first 2 miles
are dry, until you reach Bubbs Creek Bridge. Take the fork to the left
and head uphill. The first waterfall is a pretty spot to take a break.
From here, the trail meanders along the river, and through forest and
swamp areas, before it comes out at the base of Mist Falls, a wide
expanse of a waterfall that flows generously in spring. There are dozens of great picnic spots here and along the way up. Return along the
same route or, at Bubbs Creek Bridge, cross over and head back on

the Sentinel Trail, which adds a mile to the hike. From Mist Falls, you can also continue on to Paradise Valley, described below.

8 miles/2–3 hr. Moderate to strenuous. Begin at the short-term parking area at Road's End past Cedar Grove Village and follow the signs.

Muir's Rock   Okay, so you can't walk too far, don't have time, and so on. Well, now there's no excuse. This level, simple, short stroll takes you to one of the most historically significant spots in the park's modern-day history. From this wide, flat rock, John Muir used to deliver impassioned speeches about the Sierra. When referring to logging the giant trees, he said that mankind may as well "sell the rain clouds and the snow and the rivers to be cut up and carried away, if that were possible."

300 ft./10 min. Easy. The pulpit is 300 ft. from the parking area at Road's End, along the trail to Zumwalt Meadow.

Paradise Valley ★★   This makes a great overnight hike—the valley is pretty and there's much to explore—but it can also be accomplished as an ambitious day hike. Follow the Mist Falls trail to the falls and then head up 3 miles of switchbacks to Paradise Valley. The valley is 3 miles long, relatively flat, and beautiful. Hike through the valley to connect with the John Muir Trail and the rest of the backcountry, or return the way you came.

12 miles/7–10 hr. Moderate to strenuous. Begin at the short-term parking area at Road's End past Cedar Grove Village and follow the signs.

River Trail   This trail heads upstream as it hugs the river and can be shortened if you just want to walk to the waterfalls (0.5-mile round-trip) or Zumwalt Meadow (3 miles round-trip; a shorter version is listed below). The waterfalls are 0.3 miles along the trail. The falls are short but powerful—do *not* attempt to climb them. Just north of the falls, back toward the parking area, is a sign that reads ZUMWALT MEADOW—ROAD'S END. Take this trail, which initially hugs the highway before breaking off into a beautiful canyon. At 1.5 miles is the Zumwalt Bridge. If you were to cross the bridge, you'd be 0.3 miles from the Zumwalt Meadow parking area. Do not cross the bridge; instead, continue onward up the canyon for another 0.3 miles to Zumwalt Meadow. From here there's a slight incline. In 0.5 miles you'll reach a fork; keep right. The rest of the hike follows the riverbank, which sports plenty of swimming and fishing holes. After 2.5 miles, you'll come to another footbridge. Cross over and it's a short 0.5-mile walk back to the Road's End parking area, where you can try to catch a ride. Otherwise, retrace your steps back to your car.

5.5 miles/4 hr. Easy. From the Cedar Grove Ranger Station, drive 3.1 miles to the Roaring River Fall parking area.

Zumwalt Meadow ★

This hike takes you across a lovely meadow, with lots of broad views. Cross the bridge and walk left for 100 yards to a fork. Take the trail that leads to the right for a bird's-eye view of the meadow below before descending 50 feet. The trail runs along the meadow's edge, where the fragrance of ponderosa pine, sugar pine, and incense cedar fill the air. The loop returns along the banks of the South Fork of the Kings River; watch for Grand Sentinel and North Dome rising in the background.

1.5 miles/1 hr. Easy. The trail begins at the Zumwalt Meadow parking area, 1 mile west of Road's End, past Cedar Grove Village.

ELSEWHERE IN THE PARKS

Cold Springs Nature Trail (in Sequoia's Mineral King)

This easy loop showcases the natural history and beauty of the region. It passes near private cabins left over from the days before 1978, when the Mineral King area was added to Sequoia National Park. The walk offers views of the Mineral King Valley and surrounding peaks. It can get hot and dry in summer, so carry additional water.

2 miles/1 hr. Easy. Begin at Mineral King's Cold Springs Campground, across from the ranger station.

Kings River National Recreation Trail

So it's a long drive, but after a hike in upper Kings Canyon, this is a great place to see what the canyon looks like from the bottom. The views here rival anything in the park, with peaks towering overhead and the river rushing nearby. The first mile alternates between rapids and pools that offer great fishing. At 1.5 miles, you can see up Converse Creek and its rugged canyon. At 3 miles, you'll find Spring Creek, a short but pretty waterfall and a good place to rest. You can turn around here for a total hike of 6 miles, or proceed for the 10-mile option.

From this point, the trail ascends the steep Garlic Spur, a ridge that ends suddenly at the ledge of the canyon. The trail above Spring Creek is flecked with obsidian, the nearest source of which is the Mono Craters, more than 100 miles to the north. For that reason, many believe this trail was used for trading by the Monache Indians. After the long, steep ascent, the trail heads down to Garlic Meadow Creek. A short distance upstream are large pools and wide resting areas. Beyond the creek, the trail is not maintained.

6–10 miles/4–8 hr., depending on distance traveled. Easy to Spring Creek; strenuous to Garlic Meadow Creek. On CA 180, 6 miles west of Big Stump Entrance, turn north on FS Rd. 12SO1, a dirt road marked MCKENZIE HELIPORT, DELILAH LOOKOUT, CAMP 4.5 MILES. Drive 18 miles to the Kings River. Turn west and drive 2 1/2 miles to Rodgers Crossing. Cross the bridge and turn east, following signs to the Kings River Trail. The trail head is at the east end of a parking lot another 7 miles ahead, at the road's end.

Marble Fork Trail (in Sequoia's Foothills)   This is one of the most scenic hikes in the Foothills area of Sequoia National Park. The walk leads to a deep gorge, where the roaring Marble Fall spills in a cascade over multicolored boulders. From the parking area, begin hiking north up the Southern California Edison flume. After crossing the flume on a wooden bridge, watch on the right for a sign to the trail and head east uphill. The trail has some steep switchbacks and is near some large poison oak bushes that sport stems 3 inches wide. Watch out for these bare sticks in late fall and winter. The trail will then begin to flatten out and settle into a slight slope for the rest of the hike up to the waterfalls. Look for large yuccas and California bay trees along the way. After 2 miles, you'll be able to see the waterfalls as the trail cuts through white-and-gray marble. Once you reach the falls, it's almost impossible to hike any farther, so don't attempt it. The marble slabs break easily, and boulders in the area can get slick. Be extra careful when the water is high. This is a good hike year-round, but can be hot during summer. Upon your return, be sure to check yourself thoroughly for ticks.

6 miles/4–6 hr. Strenuous. Follow the dirt road at the upper end of Potwisha Campground, which is 3³/₄ miles east of the Ash Mountain Entrance. There is a small parking area past campsite no. 16.

Potwisha and River's Edge   This was the site of an American Indian village known as Potwisha, home to a tribe of Monache. The main village was just about where the dump station is now. On the bedrock are mortar holes where the women ground acorns into meal. From here, the trail continues up the river to a sandy beach and a good swimming hole. The trail turns east upstream before the suspension bridge, then northward up a short but steep hill to the road. Turn west (left) and hike the short distance back to the parking area.

0.5 miles/30 min. Easy. From the Ash Mountain Entrance, take the highway to the Potwisha Campground. At the campground entrance (which will be to your left), turn right down a paved road toward an RV dump station until it hits a dead end at a parking area. Continue toward the river on a footpath to open bedrock.

Wildman Meadow (Sequoia National Forest)   This hike through the Monarch Wilderness starts with a relatively easy trek to Deer Cove. After reaching Deer Cove, it's a steep ascent to 7,500 feet—a 1,900-foot gain in 5 miles. From Deer Cove, hike 3.5 miles to a sandy knoll and a good view into the rugged canyon drainage area of Grizzly Creek. At 6.5 miles, you'll top the ridge and cross over to the north-facing slope. A quick drop lands you in Wildman Meadow.

14 miles/10 hr. Strenuous. The trail head for Deer Cove Trail is just north of CA 180, 2¹/₂ miles west of Cedar Grove and the Kings Canyon border in the Sequoia National Forest.

2 EXPLORING THE BACKCOUNTRY

Finding quiet and solitude is not nearly as difficult here as it is in Yosemite. Mineral King and the Giant Forest in Sequoia, along with Cedar Grove in Kings Canyon, are the main points of entry into the backcountry, but the wilderness here is never farther than 5 miles in any direction. It surrounds the park, and just about any hike that lasts more than an hour will get you into the wild. The park is crisscrossed by numerous trails leading into the high country, including the world-famous Pacific Crest Trail, as well as the John Muir Trail, which begins in Yosemite and ends at Sequoia's Mount Whitney.

Mineral King, in Sequoia, is a quiet spot that attracts few people to its 11 trails because the road to the glacial valley is so difficult to drive. Avalanches have swept swaths of trees aside, and the valley floor is covered with wild meadows. Higher up, there are woods of red fir, white fir, and lodgepole pine. The landscape is rocky but colorful. Alpine trails begin at 7,500 feet and climb from there.

Cedar Grove, in Kings Canyon, is at the dead-end of CA 180. From here, to the north and east, the park is inaccessible to vehicular traffic. Hikes from Cedar Grove head out toward the Rae Lakes Loop, Monarch Wilderness, and beyond.

PREPARING FOR YOUR BACKCOUNTRY TRIP

Be sure to get a detailed topographical map before setting off on any overnight hike. Maps are available at all ranger stations and at visitor centers throughout the park. You may want to pick up a copy of a free trip-planning guide for the wilderness areas of the parks, available at park visitor centers or by calling ℭ **559/565-3766** to request one.

PERMITS & FEES   All overnight backpacking trips require a wilderness permit, available by mail, by fax, or in person at the ranger station closest to the hike you want to take. First-come, first-served permits can be issued the morning of your trip or after 1pm on the preceding afternoon. In summer, permits cost $15 per party; in winter, they're free.

Reservations can be made at least 14 days in advance, from March 1 to September 10. To reserve a permit, you must provide a name, address, telephone number, the number of people in your party, the method of travel (snowshoe, horse, foot), the number of stock if applicable, start and end dates, start and end trail heads, a principal destination, and a rough itinerary. Download the application from the park's website and mail it to **Wilderness Permit Reservations,**

Sequoia & Kings Canyon National Parks, 47050 Generals Hwy. #60, Three Rivers, CA 93271; or fax it to **559/565-4239.** Reserved permits must be picked up by 9am. If you're delayed, call the ranger station or else you risk forfeiting your permit. If your hike crosses agency boundaries, get the permit from the agency on whose land the hike begins. Only one permit is required.

For hikes beginning in Sequoia National Forest (or in Giant Sequoia National Monument, which is managed as a section of this national forest), pick up your permits at the ranger district offices in Kernville or Springville, or contact **Sequoia National Forest,** 1839 S. Newcomb St., Porterville, CA 93257 (© **559/784-1500;** www.fs.fed. us/r5/sequoia). The national forest wraps around the southern and western portions of Sequoia & Kings Canyon National Parks. Permits are free; there are no quotas on trails in this forest.

In Sierra National Forest, permits are also free, but reservations are $5 and quotas apply year-round. Permits are issued at the ranger station closest to your trail head. This forest lies west and north of Kings Canyon National Park. For maps and further information, contact **Sierra National Forest,** 1600 Tollhouse Rd., Clovis, CA 93611 (© **559/297-0706;** www.fs.fed.us/r5/sierra).

The Inyo National Forest administers areas that stretch from the Sierra Crest to Owens Valley. Most trails here have quotas, and free permits are required. Reservations are available 3 months in advance and cost $5 per person, or $15 for Mount Whitney, which are issued through a lottery. For reservations, contact **Wilderness Permit Reservations,** Inyo National Forest, 351 Pacu Lane, Ste. 200, Bishop, CA 93514 (© **760/873-2483;** 760/873-2485 for information only; fax 760/873-2484; www.fs.fed.us/r5/inyo).

Food drops can be arranged in advance, but are difficult without the help of an outfitter. No packaging from the drop may be left behind. Call the parks' wilderness office (© **559/565-3766**) for information. Food can also be mailed to the Cedar Grove and Mineral King ranger stations. Packages are held for 3 weeks from the date received or 3 weeks after the expected pickup date, whichever is longer. Use regular U.S. Mail. Address packages with your name, identification as a trail hiker, and pickup date, all on the first line. Send packages in care of the Cedar Grove Ranger Station, Box 926, Kings Canyon National Park, CA 93633, or in care of the Mineral King Ranger Station, Star Route, Three Rivers, CA 93271.

The Cedar Grove Ranger Station is usually open daily from 8am to 5pm between Memorial Day and Labor Day. The Mineral King Ranger Station is open from 8am to 4pm from Memorial Day weekend to early October.

frequent these regions. Stay off high peaks during thunderstorms, and don't attempt any climb if it looks as though a storm is rolling in; exposed peaks are often struck by lightning. In the summer months, mosquitoes and sunburn are real problems, so bring plenty of repellent and sunscreen.

OVERNIGHT HIKES

There are 14 ranger stations in the wilderness of the park. Eight are along the John Muir and Pacific Crest trails. Another six are in the southern part of the park in the Sequoia backcountry. Most are not staffed fall through spring. To find out which ranger station is closest to your trail head, consult the park map handed out free at all entrances. *Note:* Many of the following routes are buried under snow in winter.

High Sierra Trail This trail is a popular route into the backcountry. Some use it as a one-way passage to Mount Whitney. The trail gets a lot of sun, so begin early in the day. From the parking area, head out on a paved trail to the south (straight), over several bridges, and to a junction. Turn right onto the High Sierra Trail. You will pass Eagle View, the Wolverton Cutoff, and Panther Creek. Hike at least 3 miles before setting up camp. For $175 to $250 double (meals included), a civilized lodging option is the 11-mile hike from Crescent Meadow to the **Bearpaw High Sierra Camp (€ 866/807-3598;** www.visitsequoia.com).

At least 10 miles/5 hr. Strenuous. Take CA 198 to Giant Forest and proceed to Crescent Meadow Rd. Bear right at the junction, passing the signed parking area for Moro Rock. The road ends at the Crescent Meadow parking area.

Jennie Lakes Trail This is a nice overnight hike that's not too demanding and can be further extended into the Jennie Lakes Wilderness Area. From the parking area, cross through the campground and move across Big Meadow Creek. The trail climbs from here. At Fox Meadow, there is a wooden trail sign and a register for hikers to sign. At the next junction, head right toward Jennie Lake (left goes toward the Weaver Lake Trail) and up to Poop Out Pass. From here, it's a drop down to the Boulder Creek drainage area and on to emerald-green Jennie Lake. This hike can be combined with a second day hike to Weaver Lake: Just retrace your steps to the Weaver Lake turn-off. Weaver Lake is a relatively warm mountain lake surrounded by blueberry bushes that reportedly weigh heavy with fresh fruit in July. Camp at least a quarter-mile from the lakeshore.

At least 12 miles/7 hr. Moderate to strenuous. From Grant Grove, drive about 7 miles south on the Generals Hwy. to the turnoff for Big Meadows Campground. The trail head and parking are on the south side of the road next to a ranger station.

Lakes Trail   This trail moves along a string of tarns—high mountain lakes created by the scouring action of glaciers thousands of years ago. Heather Lake and Pear Lake are popular destinations along this route. From the trail head, go straight ahead (east), avoiding the Long Meadow Trail. Climb up a moraine ridge and soon you'll be hiking above Wolverton Creek, which darts through small meadows strewn with wildflowers. At a junction with the Panther Gap Trail, head left toward Heather Lake. At a second junction, you'll have to choose your direction. To the right is Hump Trail, a steep but always open trail, with no extreme drop-offs. To the left is the Watchtower Trail, which moves along a granite ledge blasted in the rock with dynamite. With the Tokopah Valley far below, the Watchtower Trail hike is not for those who suffer vertigo. Both trails wind up at Heather Lake. Camping is not allowed here, but is okay farther up the trail at Pear and Emerald lakes.

At least 13 miles/7 hr. Moderate to strenuous. From Giant Forest, drive north on the Generals Hwy. to the Wolverton parking area. The trail head is on the left of the parking lot as you enter from the highway.

3 OTHER SPORTS & ACTIVITIES

CROSS-COUNTRY SKIING   There are 35 miles of marked backcountry trails in the parks. For information, call park concessionaires (✆ **559/335-5500** in Grant Grove; ✆ **559/565-4070** in the Wuksachi Lodge area).

In Sequoia, the **Pear Lake Ski Hut** is open to the public for overnight backcountry accommodations from mid-December through April for $30 to $40 per person per night. The hut is equipped with a pellet stove and cooking gear, but guests need to bring their own food. Reservations are by a November lottery. Call ✆ **559/565-4222** for more information.

FISHING   Open all year for trout fishing—rainbow, brook, German brown, and golden trout—are the Kaweah drainage, the parks' lakes, and a section of the South Fork of the Kings River. Most other waters are open for trout fishing from late April to mid-November, and for other species year-round. California fishing licenses (available at stores in the park) are required for anglers 16 and older; you should also get a copy of the National Park Service's fishing regulations, available at visitor centers.

HORSEBACK RIDING Guided horseback and mule rides and overnight pack trips are offered by concessionaires in both parks and the adjacent national monument during the summer. In Kings Canyon, **Cedar Grove Pack Station** (℃ **559/565-3464** in summer, 337-2314 in winter) is located about 1 mile east of Cedar Grove Village, and **Grant Grove Stables** (℃ **559/335-9292** in summer, 337-2314 in winter) is located near Grant Grove Village. In Giant Sequoia National Monument, **Horse Corral Pack Station** (℃ **559/565-3404** in summer, 564-6429 in winter; www.horsecorralpackers.com) is located on Big Meadows Road, 10 miles east of Generals Highway. The pack stations offer hourly rides as well as overnight treks, while the stables offer day rides only. Rates range from $30 to $40 for a 1-hour ride to $100 to $200 for a full day in the saddle; call for current charges for pack trips.

SNOWSHOEING On winter weekends, rangers lead free introductory snowshoe hikes in **Grant Grove** (℃ **559/565-4307**) and around **Wuksachi Lodge** (℃ **559/565-4480**). Snowshoes are provided; the hikes last 2 hours.

WHITE-WATER BOATING The Kaweah and Upper Kings rivers within the parks are not open to boating (neither kayaks nor inflatable rafts), but several companies run trips on the rivers just outside the parks. You're guaranteed to get wet on this thrilling roller-coaster ride through the rapids; it's a great way not only to see these scenic rivers, but also to experience them close up.

Whitewater Voyages (℃ **800/400-7238;** www.whitewatervoyages.com) offers trips on the Kaweah, Kings, Merced, and other rivers, with rates that range from $109 to $219 for half- and full-day trips. Multiday trips are also available (call for rates). **Kings River Expeditions** (℃ **800/846-3674** or 559/233-4881; www.kingsriver.com) specializes in rafting trips on the Kings River. Day trips run $99 to $160 per person. Overnight trips are also available (call for rates).

8

Where to Stay & Eat in Sequoia & Kings Canyon

With campgrounds scattered throughout these national parks and the nearby Giant Sequoia National Monument, you should have little trouble finding a spot to pitch your tent or park your RV. However, be aware that no RV hookups are available in the parks or monument, and full-service commercial RV parks in the surrounding towns are in short supply. Those who prefer "roughing it" in comfortable hotels will find a variety of options, both within and outside the parks, ranging from inexpensive mom-and-pop–style motels to historic bed-and-breakfast inns and delightful mountain lodges. As for food, there are quite a few choices, so you should have no worries about going hungry.

The three primary gateway communities discussed in this chapter are all along CA 198. Visalia, centered around a charming downtown, is 36 miles from Sequoia National Park's Ash Mountain Entrance and the largest city in the area, with the most facilities. Closer to the parks are Lemon Cove, 11 miles from the park border, and Three Rivers, 7 miles from the park border.

Note: From several miles inside the Ash Mountain Entrance to Giant Forest, the Generals Highway is narrow and winding and not recommended for vehicles more than 22 feet long; these should enter the parks from CA 180.

1 LODGING

INSIDE THE PARKS

Accommodations within these national parks range from rustic cabins to pleasant and well-equipped motel-style lodging, usually with a mountain-lodge atmosphere and great views. There are also several good lodging choices in the nearby Giant Sequoia National Monument and in the gateway towns of Visalia, Three Rivers, and Lemon Cove (see the listings under "Outside the Parks," below).

Cedar Grove Lodge   This motel is set on the bank of the Kings
River. Getting here is half the fun—it's a 36-mile drive down a winding highway that provides beautiful vistas along the way. The rooms
are standard motel units—clean and comfortable, but nothing special. What you're really paying for is the location, surrounded by tall
trees with a pretty river running by. Most of the units are above the
snack bar and boast communal decks with river views. However, we
prefer the three smaller rooms on ground level, even though they're
not quite as attractively appointed, since they offer private patios
looking right out on the river.

CA 180 (P.O. Box 907), Cedar Grove, Kings Canyon National Park, CA 93633.
© 866/522-6966 or 559/335-5500. www.sequoia-kingscanyon.com. 18 units.
$119–$135 double. AE, DISC, MC, V. Closed Nov–Apr. **Amenities:** Restaurant (see
"Where to Eat," later in this chapter). *In room:* A/C, fridge (in ground-floor rooms).

Grant Grove Cabins Ⓥalue   Although all accommodations here
are cabins, there's a wide range of amenities and prices to be found,
from handsomely restored units that ooze historical ambience to
rustic tent-cabins that simply provide a comfortable bed out of the
weather at a very low cost. Those who want to "rough it" in style
should reserve one of the nine cabins built in the 1920s; these have
electricity, indoor plumbing, and private bathrooms. A bit less modern, but still quite comfortable, are the 43 rustic cabins that have
kerosene lanterns for light and a shared bathhouse. Some are wooden
cabins; others, available in summer only, have wood floors and walls
but canvas roofs. All units have full linen service. It's a 10-minute
walk from the cabins to the Kings Canyon Visitor Center in Grant
Grove; also nearby is the Grant Grove Restaurant (see "Where to
Eat," later in this chapter).

CA 180 (P.O. Box 907), Grant Grove Village, Kings Canyon National Park, CA 93633.
© 866/522-6966 or 559/335-5500. www.sequoia-kingscanyon.com. 53 units (9
with private bathroom). $63–$91 cabin with shared bathroom; $129–$140 cabin
with private bathroom. AE, DISC, MC, V. Register at Grant Grove Village Registration Center, btw. the restaurant and gift shop. **Amenities:** Restaurant; Wi-Fi (free).
In room: No phone.

John Muir Lodge ★   This handsome log lodge, built in 1998,
looks perfect in its beautiful national-park setting. A mountain-lodge
atmosphere prevails here. It's an excellent choice for visitors who want
quiet, comfortable, modern accommodations, with full bathrooms
and coffeemakers, situated in a forest environment. Standard rooms
offer two queen-size beds and wonderful views of the surrounding
woods. Suites consist of two connecting standard rooms, except that

one of the rooms has a queen-size bed and a queen sofa sleeper instead of two queens.

CA 180 (P.O. Box 907), Grant Grove Village, Kings Canyon National Park, CA 93633. ⓒ 866/522-6966 or 559/335-5500. www.sequoia-kingscanyon.com. 30 units. $172–$188 double. AE, DISC, MC, V. Register at Grant Grove Village Registration Center, btw. the restaurant and gift shop. **Amenities:** Wi-Fi (free, at Grant Grove Village Registration Center). *In room:* No phone.

Silver City Mountain Resort ★ Ⓕinds This is an excellent choice for those seeking a woodsy experience in a handsome cabin surrounded by forest. There are three types of cabins here, with a variety of bed combinations (some sleep up to eight) and woodstoves for heat. Blankets and pillows are provided, but guests need to bring their own sheets, pillowcases, towels, and trash bags. The top-of-the-line Swiss Chalets are finished in knotty pine with completely equipped kitchens, full bathrooms, and an outdoor barbecue. The mid-level units, dubbed Family Cabins, have two bedrooms and complete kitchens, propane wall lamps, small restrooms with toilets but no showers (there is a central bathhouse), and decks with barbecue grills. Historical Cabins, built in the 1930s, are the most basic units, with light from kerosene and propane lamps, plus a camp kitchen. Some have refrigerators, and all share the bathhouse.

Mineral King, Sequoia National Park, CA 93262. Mailing address: P.O. Box 56, Three Rivers, CA 93271. ⓒ **559/561-3223** in summer, or 805/461-3223 in winter. Fax 805/461-3116. www.silvercityresort.com. 14 cabins (7 with shared central bathhouse). $100–$395 cabin. 2- to 3-night minimum stay. Discounts offered around June 1–15 and after Sept 18. MC, V. Located 21 miles up Mineral King Rd. **Amenities:** Restaurant; Wi-Fi (free).

Wuksachi Lodge ★★ The Wuksachi Lodge is by far the most upscale lodging in Sequoia & Kings Canyon. Rooms are located in three buildings separated from the lodge by parking lots. Views out the windows are dominated by the forest and surrounding mountains. The standard units have one king-size or two queen-size beds and a small desk; deluxe rooms are larger, with two queen-size beds or a king-size and a sofa bed, plus a table and two chairs; what are called superior rooms are actually minisuites, with two queen-size beds or one king, plus a sofa bed in an alcove sitting area with a sliding door (a good place for your teenager). Another plus: A trail starting here winds 3.1 miles through the forest to Lodgepole.

CA 180 and CA 198 (P.O. Box 89), Sequoia National Park, CA 93262. ⓒ **866/807-3598** or 801/559-4930. www.visitsequoia.com. 102 units. May–Oct and holidays $194–$260; Nov–Apr $81–$115. AE, DISC, MC, V. **Amenities:** Restaurant (see "Where to Eat," later in this chapter); lounge; Wi-Fi (free). *In room:* TV, fridge, hair dryer, Internet (fee).

Additional choices can be found outside the parks' boundaries; in most cases, you'll be passing these facilities and a few others as you travel to different sections of the parks.

In Giant Sequoia National Monument

Montecito Sequoia Lodge ★ **Kids** The Montecito is a well-stocked resort that caters to families and large groups, although guests of all ages will enjoy this well-run facility. It's open year-round and offers recreation of all types—from fishing and fencing to cross-country skiing (85 miles of groomed trails begin here). There's even a small lake, offering seasonal sailing and canoeing. Recreation is more limited in winter, when options includes snowshoeing and ice skating. The recently upgraded guest rooms, which all have private bathrooms, are located in four separate buildings; 13 cabins share two bathhouses. Bed types and numbers vary, with units that sleep from two to eight. The property has a mountain-lodge atmosphere. Meals are served buffet style.

8000 Generals Hwy. (P.O. Box 858), Giant Sequoia National Monument, Kings Canyon National Park, CA 93633. ℭ **800/227-9900**, 800/843-8667, or 559/565-3388. Fax 559/565-3223. www.mslodge.com. 36 units, plus 13 cabins that share 2 bathhouses. $99–$279 double. 6-night (Sun–Fri) minimum stay in summer except Sat, when 1-night stays are allowed. Rates include all meals. AE, DISC, MC, V. Take CA 180 into Kings Canyon National Park, turn right at the fork, and drive 8 miles south to the lodge entrance, turn right, and follow the road about ¹/₂ mile to the parking lot. **Amenities:** Dining room; bar; children's and teen programs; Jacuzzi; large heated outdoor pool; 2 outdoor tennis courts; watersports equipment.

Stony Creek Lodge This small, basic lodge offers motel-style accommodations in a pretty setting in Giant Sequoia National Monument, located 20 minutes south of Grant Grove in Sequoia National Forest. The guest rooms are pleasant and sleep from two to four. There's also a sporadically open pizzeria and gas station here.

Generals Hwy. (P.O. Box 907), Giant Sequoia National Monument, Kings Canyon National Park, CA 93633. ℭ **866/522-6966** or 559/335-5500. www.sequoia-kingscanyon.com. 11 units. $149–$169 double. AE, DISC, MC, V. Closed Sept–May. Take the Stony Creek Village exit off the Generals Hwy., btw. Grant Grove Village and Wuksachi. **Amenities:** Restaurant (seasonal, sporadic hours); store.

In the Nearby Gateway Towns

In addition to the properties discussed below, reliable chains in Visalia include the **Holiday Inn,** 9000 W. Airport Dr. (ℭ **559/651-5000**), which has rates of $89 to $149 double; and the **Super 8,** 4801 W. Noble Ave. (ℭ **559/627-2885**), charging $65 to $70 double. Lodging options in Three Rivers include the **Western Holiday Lodge,**

40105 Sierra Dr. (© **559/561-4119**), which charges $89 to $199 double; and the **Comfort Inn & Suites,** 40820 Sierra Dr. (© **800/331-2140** or 559/561-9000), charging $99 to $199 double. All have lower rates in the winter.

Ben Maddox House ★   Our top choice for an enchanting place to stay in the Visalia area, the Ben Maddox House is named for one of Visalia's most prominent citizens during the late 1800s and early 1900s. Maddox started the local newspaper and the area's first electric company. The inn, located 4 blocks from downtown Visalia on a street with a number of other Victorian homes, is replete with gardens, decks, and a citrus orchard that includes a 100-year-old lemon tree that is still producing. Large palms grace the front yard. The house itself is impressive, with a large, triangular gable and a long, covered porch, where you can relax and watch the world go slowly by. The interior is furnished with antiques, including many Victorian pieces, and the comfortable and attractive guest rooms have 14-foot ceilings and white-oak floors. One unit has a California king-size bed; the rest have queen-size beds. Breakfast is a treat, featuring terrific quiches made with local veggies.

601 N. Encina St., Visalia, CA 93291. © **800/401-9800** or 559/739-0721. Fax 559/739-0729. www.benmaddoxhouse.com. 6 units, including 1 cottage. $150–$185 double; $375 cottage. Rates include full breakfast. AE, DISC, MC, V. **Amenities:** Large outdoor pool; Wi-Fi (free). *In room:* TV/VCR or DVD, fridge, hair dryer.

Buckeye Tree Lodge ★   Located just a quarter-mile from the entrance to Sequoia National Park, this motel offers affordable and attractive rooms, not to mention rolling lawns that end at a picturesque river. Every unit has a patio or balcony offering splendid views of the main fork of the Kaweah River. Accommodations are clean, basic motel units. Eight units have showers only; the rest have tub/shower combos.

46000 Sierra Dr., Three Rivers, CA 93271. © **559/561-5900.** www.buckeyetree.com. 12 units. $120–$136 double; lower rates in winter. Rates include continental breakfast. MC, V. Pets accepted ($10/night). **Amenities:** Outdoor pool. *In room:* A/C, TV/DVD, DVD library, fridge, Wi-Fi (free).

Lake Elowin Resort (Finds   One of our favorite places to stay in the Sierra, this quirky resort is exactly what a national-park lodging should be—a place to get away from it all. There are no phones and no TVs, just rustic but clean cabins nestled under huge trees, all looking out at Lake Elowin, a small body of water above the Kaweah River. Milton Melkonian purchased the 1920s-era resort in the 1970s with the idea of creating a place to coexist with nature; it now attracts all sorts of creative types, as well as anyone seeking an escape. Cabins can accommodate two to six people. We especially like cabin no. 1, sitting close to the lake with a delightful view, and the Master Cabin, boasting a fireplace, deck, and Jacuzzi. All cabins include linens and towels, cookware, barbecues, and canoes—just bring food, sunblock, and a good attitude.

43840 Dineley Dr., Three Rivers, CA 93271. ☎ **559/561-3460.** Fax 559/561-1300. www.lake-elowin.com. 10 cabins (all with shower only). $120–$145 double; $130–$195 cabin; $225 Master Cabin. AE, DISC, MC, V. From eastbound Sierra Dr. in Three Rivers, about 2¹⁄₂ miles before the park entrance, turn left on Dineley Dr. (the street sign says DINLEY) and drive across a bridge. Bear right, and it's less than ¹⁄₂ mile to the resort's driveway. **Amenities:** Swimming hole. *In room:* A/C, kitchen, no phone.

Plantation Bed & Breakfast ★

Step out of the Sierra Nevada and into the Old South at this fun B&B, where inspiration comes straight from *Gone With the Wind*. Honeymooners might enjoy the luxurious Scarlett O'Hara Room, with a king-size bed, velvet love seat, fireplace, and marble bathroom with Jacuzzi and separate shower. Our favorite, though, is the Belle Watling Room, done up in an elegant bordello style, with a king-size bed and an enormous mirror, a red crystal chandelier, and a claw-foot bathtub painted with a tasteful nude. Two rooms have showers only, while the others have showers and tubs. Secluded in an orange grove are a large swimming pool and a Jacuzzi, which are available at all hours. The wonderful breakfasts include fresh fruit, homemade granola, and a hot entree such as mushroom asparagus crepes.

33038 CA 198, Lemon Cove, CA 93244. ☎ **800/240-1466** or 559/597-2555. Fax 559/597-2551. www.plantationbnb.com. 7 units. $149–$239 double. Rates include full breakfast. AE, DC, DISC, MC, V. Located on CA 198, 16 miles west of the park entrance. **Amenities:** Large pool; Jacuzzi; Wi-Fi (free). *In room:* TV/VCR (most rooms), no phone.

Sequoia Village Inn ★

The sister property of the Buckeye Tree Lodge (described above) across the street, the Sequoia Village Inn offers charming cabin-style units that sleep 2 to 12. Stylishly decorated with lodgepole bed frames and hardwood floors, they're great for couples and families alike. Many feature full kitchens and decks with great views; the smaller units have microwaves and fridges only.

43175 Sierra Dr., Three Rivers, CA 93271. ☎ **559/561-3652.** www.sequoiavillage inn.com. 10 units. $113–$319 double; lower rates in winter. AE, DC, DISC, MC, V. **Amenities:** Outdoor pool. *In room:* A/C, TV/VCR or DVD, kitchen, Wi-Fi (free, some rooms).

Visalia Marriott ★

The best hotel in Visalia—located a block off bustling Main Street—offers reliable Marriott service and style in its rooms and facilities. The property underwent a major renovation that concluded in 2007, and it shows. The rooms are chic and comfortable; units on the eighth floor feature private balconies and great city views.

300 S. Court St., Visalia, CA 93291. (©) **559/636-1111.** Fax 559/636-8224. www. visaliamarriotthotel.com. 195 units, including 7 suites. $109–$169 double; $169–$299 suite. AE, DISC, MC, V. **Amenities:** Restaurant (steakhouse); bar; concierge; exercise room; outdoor pool. *In room:* A/C, TV, hair dryer, Wi-Fi (free).

2 CAMPING

There are numerous camping opportunities both within and surrounding Sequoia & Kings Canyon National Parks. Brief descriptions of individual campgrounds follow, and you'll find additional details in the campground chart on p. 134.

It's important to remember that when camping in this area, proper food storage is *required* for the sake of the black bears in the parks as well as your safety. See local bulletin boards for instructions.

Note: You'll need a wilderness permit to stay overnight in the backcountry; see "Exploring the Backcountry" in chapter 7.

IN SEQUOIA NATIONAL PARK

The only campgrounds in the national park that accept reservations are Dorst Creek and Lodgepole (© **877/444-6777;** www.recreation. gov), which take them up to 6 months in advance; the other campgrounds are first-come, first-served. Additional information on the national park campgrounds (but not reservations) can be obtained by calling the general Sequoia & Kings Canyon information line at © **559/565-3341.**

The two biggest campgrounds in the park are in the Lodgepole area. The **Lodgepole Campground,** which has flush toilets, is often crowded, but it's pretty and not far from some spectacular big trees. Nearby backcountry trails offer some solitude. Close to the campground are a grocery store, restaurant, visitor center, children's nature center, evening ranger programs, and gift shop. From Giant Forest Museum, drive 5 miles northeast on the Generals Highway. **Dorst Creek Campground,** located 14 miles northwest of Giant Forest via the Generals Highway, is a high-elevation campground that offers easy access to Muir Grove and some pleasant backcountry trails. It has flush toilets and evening ranger programs. Group campsites are also available here by reservation.

In the Foothills area, the small **Potwisha Campground** has well-spaced sites tucked beneath oak trees along the Marble Fork of the Kaweah River. The campground has flush toilets. Note that it does get hot in summer here. From the Ash Mountain Entrance, drive 3 miles northeast on the Generals Highway to the campground entrance. The **Buckeye Flat Campground ★**, which is open to tents only, is also set among oaks along the Middle Fork of the Kaweah River, and although it also gets hot in summer, it is among our favorites due to its scenic beauty. It has flush toilets. From the Ash Mountain Entrance, drive about 6 miles northeast on the Generals Highway to the Hanging Rock Picnic Area. From here, follow signs to the campground, which is several miles down a narrow, winding road. **South Fork Campground** is the smallest and most remote campground in the park, located just inside Sequoia's southwestern boundary. It is set along the South Fork of the Kaweah River and has pit toilets only. From the town of Three Rivers, go east on South Fork Road 23 miles to the campground. The campground is free November through April.

The two campgrounds in the Mineral King area are open to tents only—no RVs or trailers. **Atwell Mill Campground** is a small but pretty campground near the East Fork of the Kaweah River, at Atwell Creek. It has pit toilets. From Three Rivers, take Mineral King Road east for 20 miles to the campground. **Cold Springs Campground,** which also has pit toilets, is a beautiful place to stay—it's just not very accessible. Once you get here, however, you'll be rewarded with beautiful scenery. It's also a good starting point for many backcountry hikes, as it's near the Mineral King Ranger Station. From Three Rivers, take Mineral King Road east for 25 miles to the campground.

IN KINGS CANYON NATIONAL PARK

All of the campgrounds in Kings Canyon are first-come, first-served only (reservations are not available), and all have flush toilets. Additional information can be obtained by calling the general Sequoia & Kings Canyon information line at © **559/565-3341.**

In the Grant Grove area, there are three attractive campgrounds near the big trees: **Azalea, Crystal Springs,** and **Sunset.** All have a nice woodsy feel, are close to park facilities, and offer evening ranger programs. To get to them from the Big Stump Entrance, take CA 180 east about 1¾ miles.

Several pleasant campgrounds lie in the Cedar Grove Village area, all accessible from CA 180, and all fairly close to the facilities in Cedar Grove Village. **Sentinel,** the first to open for the season, tends to fill up quickly. **Moraine** is the farthest from the crowds. **Sheep Creek,** located along picturesque Sheep Creek, is generally open on an as-needed basis.

Sequoia & Kings Canyon Campgrounds

CAMPGROUND	ELEV. (FT.)	TOTAL SITES	RV HOOKUPS	DUMP STATION	TOILETS	DRINKING WATER	SHOWERS	FIRE PITS/ GRILLS	LAUNDRY	PUBLIC PHONES	RESERVATIONS POSSIBLE	FEES	OPEN
INSIDE SEQUOIA NATIONAL PARK													
Atwell Mill	6,650	21	0	No	Yes	Yes	No	Yes	No	No	No	$12	Late May to Oct
Buckeye Flat	2,800	28	0	No	Yes	Yes	No	Yes	No	No	No	$18	Apr to early Sept
Cold Springs	7,500	31	0	No	Yes	Yes	No	Yes	No	No	No	$12	Late May to Oct
Dorst Creek	6,700	204	0	Yes	Yes	Yes	No	Yes	No	Yes	Yes	$20	Late June to mid-Sept
Lodgepole	6,700	204	0	Yes	Yes	Yes	Yes	Yes	Yes	Yes	Yes	$18–$20	All year
Porwisha	2,100	42	0	Yes	Yes	Yes	No	Yes	No	Yes	No	$18	All year
South Fork	3,600	10	0	No	Yes	No	No	Yes	No	No	No	$12	All year
INSIDE KINGS CANYON NATIONAL PARK													
Azalea	6,500	110	0	No	Yes	Yes	Yes	Yes	No	Yes	No	$10–$18	All year
Crystal Springs	6,500	50	0	No	Yes	Yes	Yes	Yes	No	Yes	No	$18	May–Sept
Moraine	4,600	120	0	No	Yes	Yes	Yes	Yes	Yes	Yes	No	$18	May–Oct
Sentinel	4,600	82	0	No	Yes	Yes	Yes	Yes	Yes	Yes	No	$18	Late Apr to Oct
Sheep Creek	4,600	111	0	No	Yes	Yes	Yes	Yes	Yes	No	No	$14	May to mid-Nov
Sunset	6,500	157	0	No	Yes	Yes	Yes	Yes	Yes	No	No	$18	May to mid-Sept

OUTSIDE THE PARKS												
Big Meadows	7,600	25	0	No	Yes	No	No	Yes	No	Yes	No	Free	May–Oct
Horse Creek	300	80	0	Yes	Yes	Yes	Yes	Yes	Yes	Yes	Yes	$16	All year
Hume Lake	5,200	74	0	No	Yes	Yes	No	Yes	No	Yes	Yes	$20	May–Oct
Landslide	5,800	9	0	No	Yes	No	No	Yes	No	No	No	$16	May–Oct
Lemon Cove	500	55	40	Yes	Yes	Yes	Yes	Yes	Yes	Yes	Yes	$25–$35	All year
Princess	5,900	90	0	Yes	Yes	Yes	No	Yes	No	No	Yes	$18	May–Oct
Stony Creek	6,400	49	0	No	Yes	Yes	Yes	Yes	No	Yes	Yes	$20	May–Oct
Tenmile	5,800	13	0	No	Yes	No	No	Yes	No	Yes	No	$16	May–Oct

The U.S. Forest Service operates a number of campgrounds in **Giant Sequoia National Monument,** a 327,769-acre section of Sequoia National Forest, which was given national monument status by U.S. President Bill Clinton in April 2000. These sites provide a delightful forest camping experience and are usually less crowded than the national park campgrounds. There is also primitive camping available—no fee, no facilities.

In the Hume Lake area, all of the forest service campgrounds have pit toilets except the beautiful **Hume Lake Campground,** which is set on the banks of the lake and has flush toilets. It's about 3 miles south of CA 180 via Hume Lake Road. The largest campground in this area is **Princess Campground,** located along CA 180. Two smaller options, both beyond Hume Lake via Ten Mile Road, are **Landslide Campground** and **Tenmile Campground.**

In the Stony Creek/Big Meadows area, you'll find vault toilets at all U.S. Forest Service campgrounds except **Stony Creek Campground,** located off Generals Highway in Stony Creek Village, which has flush toilets. Among the larger choices in this area is **Big Meadows Campground,** which is set along Big Meadows Creek. Nearby trails lead to the Jennie Lakes Wilderness. From Grant Grove Village, drive 7 miles southeast on the Generals Highway; then turn east on Big Meadows Road and drive 5 miles to the campground.

There are also several smaller, primitive campgrounds here; you can get information about all of the forest service campgrounds by contacting Giant Sequoia National Monument, Sequoia National Forest, Hume Lake Ranger District, 35860 E. Kings Canyon Rd., Dunlap, CA 93621 (𝄯 **559/338-2251;** www.r5.fs.fed.us/sequoia). You can make reservations at Hume Lake, Princess, or Stony Creek during the summer by calling 𝄯 **877/444-6777** or visiting www. recreation.gov.

Another great place to camp is **Horse Creek Campground,** operated by the U.S. Army Corps of Engineers. It's located along the south shore of Lake Kaweah, in Lake Kaweah Recreation Area, about 6 miles east of the community of Lemon Cove off CA 198. The lake, which is about 5 miles long and a half-mile wide, covers 1,900 acres when full and is popular with boaters, who take to the water in kayaks, canoes, personal watercraft, fishing boats, and larger patio boats. There are several boat ramps, and boat rentals are available at the **Kaweah Marina** (𝄯 **559/597-2526;** www.kaweahmarina.com); call for current rates and availability. This is also a popular fishing lake, where you're apt to catch largemouth bass, crappie, bluegill, catfish, and rainbow trout. The number of campsites varies with the water level, with the fewest usually in spring, when the lake is at its highest;

Tips **Camping in Style**

New in 2006, the luxury **Sequoia High Sierra Camp** (✆ **866/ 654-2877;** www.sequoiahighsierracamp.com), in Giant Sequoia National Monument, looks to one-up its Yosemite counterparts in terms of upscale "roughing it." For $250 per person, you get 330-square-foot bungalows with plush furnishings and three "California-cuisine-style" meals a day. Guests can choose to drive to a trail head and hike 1 mile or take an 11-mile trail. For $175 to $250 double (meals included), a less tony—but still quite civilized—option is the **Bearpaw High Sierra Camp** (✆ **866/807-3598;** www.visit sequoia.com), an 11-mile hike from Crescent Meadow in Sequoia National Park proper. Bearpaw is open June through September; Sequoia stays open into October.

many sites are underwater here until mid-July. Some are shady sites and some open, and most have good views across the lake. Flush toilets are available. For information, contact the U.S. Army Corps of Engineers, Lake Kaweah Recreation Area, P.O. Box 44270, Lemon Cove, CA 93244 (✆ **559/597-2301**). Campsite reservations are available by calling ✆ **877/444-6777** or visiting www.recreation.gov.

Those seeking a full-service commercial campground with RV hookups and all the usual amenities should head to **Lemon Cove/ Sequoia Campground,** on the west side of Lemon Cove at 32075 Sierra Dr. (✆ **559/597-2346;** www.lemoncovesequoiacamp.com). This attractive and convenient campground, located in the foothills of the Sierra Nevada (22 miles east of U.S. 99), can handle both tents and large rigs with slide-outs. It offers cable TV hookups, propane sales, a convenience store, grassy and shaded sites, a recreation room, a playground and volleyball court, and an outdoor swimming pool.

3 WHERE TO EAT

Major improvements and additions to the restaurant scene in these parks in recent years mean that, yes, you can have a really good meal, or, if you prefer, find a quick and tasty lunch at a fairly reasonable price. In addition, there are several good possibilities in the communities outside the parks as well as within the Giant Sequoia National Monument.

Every Wednesday through Sunday from mid-June to early August, an all-you-can-eat **barbecue** takes place in the beautiful outdoor setting of Wolverton Meadow, just south of Lodgepole in Sequoia National Park. Tickets can be purchased at the Wuksachi Lodge or Lodgepole Market. Call © **866/807-3598** for information.

There is also a seasonal **pizzeria** at Stony Creek Lodge, on Generals Highway between Grant Grove and Wuksachi, that serves lunch and dinner.

Cedar Grove Snack Bar AMERICAN   The only dining option at Cedar Grove offers a simple but adequate menu at affordable prices, although those staying at the lodge here for several days will quickly tire of the limited choices. The cafe has pleasant outdoor balcony seating that overlooks the river.

Cedar Grove, Kings Canyon National Park. © **559/565-0100.** Breakfast $4–$10; lunch and dinner main courses $5–$20. AE, DISC, MC, V. Mid-June to mid-Aug daily 7am–2pm and 5–8pm; mid-May to mid-June and mid-Aug to mid-Oct Mon–Fri 8–10:30am, Sat–Sun 8am–2pm, daily 5–7pm. Closed mid-Oct to mid-May.

Grant Grove Restaurant Kids AMERICAN   This pleasant cafe-style restaurant, located in the hub of activity in Kings Canyon National Park, is the primary option for a sit-down meal, with good service and a simple but very adequate menu. Breakfast and lunch are typical American fare, including pizza—always a favorite with kids. Complete dinners include steaks, pastas, chicken, and trout dishes.

Grant Grove Village, Kings Canyon National Park. © **559/335-5500,** ext. 305. Breakfast and lunch $5–$15; dinner main courses $8–$30. AE, DISC, MC, V. Late May to early Sept daily 7am–2pm and 5–9pm; early Sept to late May daily 9am–2pm and 5–7pm (until 8pm Fri–Sat).

Lodgepole Market Value DELI/PIZZA   The Watchtower Deli and the Harrison BBQ & Grill are actually two separate counter-service, fast-food restaurants in the Lodgepole Market Center. At the snack bar, you'll find kids' favorites such as burgers, hot dogs, and pizza. Healthier fare is available at the deli, which specializes in made-to-order sandwiches, wraps, and salads—and ice cream.

Lodgepole, Sequoia National Park. © **559/565-3301.** Most items $4–$13. AE, MC, V. Daily 8am–8pm. Snack bar open year-round, with shorter hours fall–spring; deli closed Nov–Apr.

Wuksachi Dining Room ★★ AMERICAN   A wood-beamed ceiling, huge stone fireplace, and large windows offering wonderful views of the surrounding forest make this upscale lodge-style restaurant a delightful spot for a refined and relaxing meal. Standard American breakfast buffets are the morning fare, while a number of salads and sandwiches—such as a half-pound burger or citrus-marinated salmon with caramelized onion—are offered during lunch and dinner. The dinner entrees are both creative and elegant, with a nice mix of meat and potatoes, seafood, and vegetarian fare.

Wuksachi Lodge, Sequoia National Park. © **559/565-4070,** ext. 608. Reservations required for dinner. Breakfast and lunch $5–$15; dinner main courses $16–$33. AE, DISC, MC, V. Daily 7–10am, 11:30am–2:30pm, and 5–10pm.

OUTSIDE THE PARKS

About 20 miles west of Kings Canyon on Generals Highway, **Clingan's Junction,** 35591 E. Kings Canyon Rd. (© **559/338-0160**), has been a standby since 1938, serving up eggs Benedict, burgers, chicken sandwiches, and steaks. In Three Rivers, **Serrano's,** 40869 Sierra Dr. (© **559/561-7283**), is a good family-run Mexican restaurant with spicy salsa and tasty carne asada.

Anne Lang's Emporium DELI A great spot for a quick lunch or picnic fare before heading into the park. This busy, full-service deli has a half-dozen or so tables inside, in a cafe-like atmosphere, plus a large deck out back (away from the highway) that overlooks the Kaweah River. After you order at the counter, the staff will prepare your sandwich to eat in or take away as a box lunch. In addition to the usual cold deli sandwiches, there are a few hot items, including burgers and chicken-breast sandwiches. You'll also find several luncheon salads, a soup of the day, fresh-baked items, ice cream, and specialty drinks including espressos, smoothies, and Italian sodas.

41651 Sierra Dr. (CA 198), Three Rivers. © **559/561-4937.** Most items $3–$7. AE, DISC, MC, V. Mon–Fri 10am–4pm; Sat–Sun 11am–4pm. Store/ice-cream parlor Mon–Fri 9am–5pm; Sat–Sun 9am–5:30pm.

Brewbaker's Restaurant & Brewery ★ Finds BREWPUB A top-notch microbrewery in downtown Visalia, the brass bar at Brewbaker's is literally within arm's reach of the huge fermentation vats. Brick walls, stained glass, and a social vibe round out the atmosphere. The beers are uniformly fantastic, while the food—including burgers, chili, fish and chips, and personal pizzas—is the best deal in town. Not only does this place brew beer, but it also makes its soda pop in house, in such flavors as orange and bubble gum. There are seating areas upstairs and down, as well as on the second-story deck with a great city view out back.

219 E. Main St., Visalia. © **559/627-2739.** www.brewbakersbrewingco.com. Main courses $7–$22. AE, DISC, MC, V. Daily 11:30am–10pm. Bar open later.

Tommy's ★★ NEW AMERICAN With a contemporary design and a menu to match, Tommy's is the most creative restaurant in Visalia. Diverse influences show up from the South (in appetizers like fried green tomatoes), the Far East (Kobe burgers), and the Rocky Mountains (Colorado rack of lamb). We particularly enjoyed the root-beer-glazed pork chop, served with a baked yam, as well as the side of bacon mac 'n' cheese and the make-your-own s'mores for dessert. The restaurant prides itself on its hand-cut Angus beef steaks, aged for at least 21 days, grilled, and finished with steak butter. There is a full bar and a California-centric wine list.

130 N. Encina St., Visalia. ⓒ **559/627-6075.** www.tommysdowntown.com. Main courses $19–$38. AE, MC, V. Tues–Thurs 5–9pm; Fri–Sat 5–10pm. Bar open later.

Vintage Press ★★ ⓕinds AMERICAN/CONTINENTAL A good pick for a romantic dinner, this stalwart's three dining rooms are elegant in the spirit of an upscale gin mill in Gold Rush–era San Francisco, featuring a handsome old bar imported from the city by the bay, plus many antiques and leaded mirrors. There's patio dining, too. The menu features several steaks alongside such dishes as sautéed shrimp scampi and crispy veal sweetbreads with a port/jalapeño/blue-cheese sauce. There are also exotic appetizers like escargot, goat-cheese rellenos, and ahi-halibut ceviche. Lunch brings smaller steaks, sandwiches, pastas, and salads. The restaurant's wine cellar offers more than 1,000 selections.

216 N. Willis St., Visalia. ⓒ **559/733-3033.** Reservations recommended for dinner. Main courses $10–$17 lunch, $18–$37 dinner. AE, DC, MC, V. Mon–Sat 11:30am–2pm and 5:30–10pm; Sun 10am–2pm and 5–9pm.

PICNIC & CAMPING SUPPLIES

Stores throughout the parks stock some basic camping supplies, such as flashlights, canteens, and tarps, plus enough food that you won't starve, but you'll find better selections in the nearby towns.

Within the parks, most of the stores are open daily from 8am until 7 or 8pm. The **Cedar Grove Market** is open May through September only, as is the **Lodgepole Market,** which has the widest selection available, including a good deli for takeout sandwiches (see above). The **Grant Grove Market** is open from 8am to 9pm May through August and from 8am to 7pm September through April. During the winter, a small selection of goods is available at **Wuksachi Lodge,** in Sequoia.

For the best selection and prices on foodstuffs outside the parks, stop in Visalia at **Save Mart,** 1591 E. Noble St., at CA 198 and Ben Maddox Way (ⓒ **559/636-0328**), on your way to the parks. This is an excellent supermarket with a good bakery and a deli that serves made-to-order sandwiches. Just east of it is a **Wal-Mart,** at 1819 E. Noble Ave. (ⓒ **559/636-2302**).

9

A Nature Guide to Yosemite and Sequoia & Kings Canyon National Parks

Yosemite and Sequoia & Kings Canyon are parks in transition. They have long been geologic wonderlands, rarities that recently ran headlong into myriad social concerns. Now the National Park Service, environmental groups, and various watchdogs are all taking a serious look at the parks' futures.

1 THE LANDSCAPE

Towering sheets of granite. Lush forests that give way to emerald meadows blanketed in wildflowers. Views that stretch farther than some countries and make visitors feel like they are standing on the edge of the world. The varied landscapes of these parks are memorable, to say the least. Yosemite has an almost bizarre conglomeration of sheer granite monoliths and wide-open spaces. Sequoia & Kings Canyon have trees that are as wide at the base as some homes, along with wildflowers in almost every patch of sun. All these wonders occur because of the area's astounding geological nature.

About 300 million years ago, layers of sediment that had been building up on the ocean floor were forced under the emerging North American continent. The process created such intense heat that the sediment became molten magma, some of which erupted via volcanoes. Where it chilled and hardened before reaching the surface, the magma created huge slabs of granite.

This process continued intermittently for about 150 million years, forming a large mountain range roughly parallel to the West Coast—the Sierra Nevada. For the next 55 million years, wind and water ate away at the volcanoes and sedimentary rock, sweeping it into California's Central Valley and leaving mountains of exposed granite.

Scientists theorize earthquakes along the present-day San Andreas Fault began forcing the eastern edge of a landmass beneath the Sierra upward 25 million years ago, eventually tipping west, raising tall mountain peaks. In Yosemite, the upheaval raised the park's eastern range to 11,000 feet, while in Sequoia & Kings Canyon, it created the ominously barren and beautiful Kaweah Ridge, also known as the Great Western Divide, which ranges from about 11,000 to 14,000 feet in elevation.

As rivers raged through the valleys, they carved deeper and deeper into the earth, eroding the bedrock. Great canyons were formed, and when the earth's temperature cooled about 3 million years ago, glaciers covered the Sierra Nevada. These fields of ice tore at the granite, expanding and contracting with such force that they carved deep valleys, slicing granite walls vertically into the steep U-shapes of Yosemite Valley and Kings Canyon.

When the glaciers melted, they left behind steep mountains smoothed by ice, along with piles of debris that dammed the flow of rivers, creating lakes in the valleys. The rest of the landscaping took place in an evolutionary blink of an eye. Over the course of 10,000 years, sediment, swept down from above, filled these lakes. Meadows were formed, and then came wildflowers, followed by trees, and eventually people.

You can still see **glaciers** in Yosemite, near Tuolumne Meadows. Also check out the glaciers on Yosemite's Mount Lyell, Mount Dana, and Mount Maclure. The glaciers here were probably formed about 2,500 years ago, but are quickly receding today.

Glaciers are responsible for the variety of **rock formations** in the parks. There are spires, domes, sheets, and arches. Yosemite has cornered the market for number and diversity, offering one or more of each within the span of an easy 3-mile walk. Most of the unusual rock landmarks here were created by fractures within the rock. These fractures occur vertically, horizontally, and at an incline. Called **joints,** they represent the weakest point of a rock and a point that has already been broken. The type of joint most common in Yosemite, and also evident in Sequoia & Kings Canyon, is sheeting. Concentric joints— fractures that seem to occur along curved lines—form after years of increasing and decreasing pressure from overlaying rock. When pressure decreases, the granite expands upward and breaks or fractures off in sheets, similar to peeling an onion very slowly.

Erratic boulders are another common sight. These large rocks were originally located elsewhere but were transported and plopped down haphazardly—again, probably by glaciers.

Ridges of rocky deposits are called **moraines,** left behind as glaciers recede. The best place to see moraines is in Yosemite, en route from Tuolumne Meadows to Tioga Pass.

The most famous rocks in Yosemite are Half Dome and El Capitan. Although **Half Dome** was probably never a full dome like North Dome, which it faces, geologists believe that about 20% of the original rock was sheared off by glaciers. The face looks smooth and slippery but is actually filled with ledges and ridges, making it a rock climber's paradise. Similar ridges exist on the dome side, enabling hikers to climb to the top (see chapter 4). Although it looks small, the top measures 13 acres. Half Dome is 8,842 feet above sea level and towers roughly 4,800 feet above the valley floor, the highest point in Yosemite Valley.

El Capitan is on the left, or north, side of the valley as you enter. It rises 3,593 feet above the valley floor and 7,569 feet above sea level. Toward the top of El Cap, the slope of the rock actually increases and hangs over the valley floor. Called the nose, it's a particular challenge for rock climbers. Look for climbers on the face, as well as off to the sides of El Cap; it's where many experts ascend and beginners learn the ropes. It takes around 4 to 7 days to climb El Capitan. The first climber reached the summit in 1958, after 47 days. The rock is also home to a pair of peregrine falcons that nest here in spring and summer.

To the east of El Cap are the **Three Brothers**—three outcroppings of rock called Lower Brother, Middle Brother, and Eagle Peak. The rocks appear to be riding piggyback and were formed by parallel fractures on an incline.

The **Cathedral Spires** are directly opposite El Cap, on the other side of the valley. They will appear before you if you turn your back to El Cap and look carefully—the rock is almost camouflaged by the valley wall beyond. Somehow these, and other spires in the park, have withstood nature's evolutionary barrage.

Another spire, this one known as **Lost Arrow,** is east of Yosemite Falls, below Yosemite Point. Look for the waterfalls to the north of Yosemite Lodge. The outcropping of rock to the east is **Yosemite Point.** Lost Arrow is an independent spire in the same area.

Continue moving east to see the **Royal Arches,** a series of 1,500-foot half-circles carved out of the rock, to the north of the Ahwahnee hotel. The Arches provide an inside view of the exfoliation process that formed many of Yosemite's domes. Here, the material that was once above the arches eroded away, taking pressure off the rock below, which expanded and cracked parallel to the surface. During particularly wet springs, water cascades over the arches in great sheets.

Above the arches is **North Dome,** the smooth, slightly lopsided dome mentioned earlier. It rises 3,562 feet above the valley floor. Nearby is **Washington Column,** a spire with a tip 1,920 feet above the valley floor. Ahwahnee Indian legend has it that a man and

(Fun Facts)   **The Life & Times of John Muir**

Over the course of his illustrious 75 years, John Muir earned a nickname: "Father of Our National Parks." In the late 19th century, he pushed for conservation of the pristine wilderness and helped establish Yosemite and Sequoia & Kings Canyon as national parks.

Born in Scotland in 1838, Muir emigrated with his family to Wisconsin at the age of 11. After an accident nearly blinded him about a decade later, he dropped everything to pursue his fascination with the natural world and decided to go to the Amazon—on foot. He didn't make it, but traveling became a way of life for Muir, and his journeys eventually took him west. He discovered the Sierra Nevada area in 1868 and worked as a shepherd in the Yosemite area. He later ran a sawmill nearby.

Muir began writing about the Sierra Nevada the moment he arrived, and his passionate words started finding an audience in the late 1800s. He wrote a number of books, contributed to numerous periodicals, and became a leading voice in the budding environmentalist movement. In 1892, Muir

woman who lived in the valley long ago fought so often that it upset the spirits. The unhappy couple was turned to stone and separated by Tenaya Creek. He is North Dome, with Washington Column as his walking stick. She is Half Dome, and if you look at it closely, a woman's profile faces northeast. Legend also has it that the streak of lighter rock between her cheek and nose was caused by a stream of tears.

Domes and impressive geologic formations appear outside the valley as well. Most are in Yosemite's high country, en route to Tuolumne Meadows, and foremost is **Olmsted Point,** an overlook that gives visitors a chance to see the granite Tenaya Canyon. Cloud's Rest and the rear of Half Dome are two distinct shapes easily recognizable from Olmsted Point, which is 9 miles west of Tuolumne Meadows.

Tuolumne Meadows itself is ringed with domes and peaks, many of which are an easier climb than the ones rising above the valley.

helped found the Sierra Club. In 1903, he took Teddy Roosevelt camping in the Yosemite backcountry and catalyzed Roosevelt's vision of an entire system of national parks.

Muir is a legend for not only his words and his deeds, but also because he was something of an eccentric. He never shaved, making way for an impressive beard. He experienced nature to its fullest—he climbed a tree during an incredible storm, sledded down Yosemite Valley's steep walls on his rump to avoid an avalanche, and chased a bear so he could study the animal's stride. (Not surprisingly, these actions have since been banned by the National Park Service.)

From the first moment a politician pondered Hetch Hetchy Reservoir, Muir fought it. Damming and drowning a place whose beauty rivaled that of Yosemite Valley was sacrilege to him. But San Francisco needed water to drink, and Congress passed legislation approving Hetch Hetchy Reservoir in 1913. John Muir died the very next year—some say of a broken heart.

In Sequoia National Park, **Moro Rock** is a dome towering 6,725 feet above sea level. Moro Rock's summit offers breathtaking views of the Kaweah Ridge, with some peaks rising to 14,000 feet.

Kings Canyon National Park boasts **North Dome,** above Cedar Grove. Some people with a vivid imagination say it resembles Half Dome. North Dome is not accessible by car or on foot.

Waterfalls hang over the Yosemite Valley like a sparkling diamond necklace. The valley boasts three of the world's tallest waterfalls. Upon entering the valley, you'll spot the 620-foot **Bridalveil Fall** first. It looks large, but that's because you haven't seen the rest of the cast.

The real biggie is **Yosemite Falls,** close to Yosemite Lodge. The fall appears to be one drop but is, in fact, a set of waterfalls that measures a combined 2,425 feet. Lower Yosemite Fall drops 320 feet; Upper Yosemite Fall descends 1,430 feet; and a cascade in the middle makes up the difference.

To the west of El Capitan you'll find **Ribbon Fall,** which drops an uninterrupted 1,612 feet to the valley floor but is often dry in summer.

The longest single fall in Yosemite is **Sentinel Fall.** It drops 2,000 feet from the west side of Sentinel Rock, directly across the valley floor from Yosemite Falls. To view this waterfall, walk back toward El Cap and make an about-face—it's one of the geology-obscured views in the park.

Up the valley are a series of dramatic staircase falls accessible only on foot. **Vernal Fall** and **Nevada Fall** occur just a half-mile apart along the same river.

Waterfalls in Sequoia & Kings Canyon are less numerous but still impressive. **Mist Falls,** in Kings Canyon, is beautiful but requires a 4-mile hike (see chapter 7). This wide waterfall near Cedar Grove is up a rushing creek, which includes several large cascades.

Below is **Roaring River Fall,** a length of waterfall also accessible only on foot; it flows from Cloud and Deadman canyons. **Garlic Fall,** in the Monarch Wilderness area just outside Kings Canyon, can be viewed from the Yucca Point overlook on CA 180.

A note on waterfalls: Most are fed by snowmelt and rely on winter runoff to survive. In late summer, many of them (including Yosemite Falls) dry up.

2 THE FLORA

There are more than 1,500 types of plants in Yosemite and Sequoia & Kings Canyon, and describing them all would fill this book. With species ranging from tiny lichen to giant sequoias, the flora in all of the parks is similar, varying primarily by elevation.

TREES

The trees native to the region consist mostly of conifers and broadleaf trees. Conifers have needles and cones, do not shed during cooler months, and maintain their green year-round, earning the name *evergreen.* Broadleaf trees drop their leaves in fall and bloom anew in spring.

At lower elevations, the two most common pines you'll find are the ponderosa pine and Jeffrey pine (both also known as "yellow pines"). The **ponderosa pine** has yellow-orange bark, needles grouped in threes, and bark scales that fit together like a jigsaw puzzle. The trunk of a ponderosa pine can grow up to 6 feet in diameter. The **Jeffrey pine** is similar to the ponderosa but tends to live at higher elevations.

The **sugar pine** grows at slightly higher elevations and can be seen along many hikes. These pines produce large pine cones, have short needles grouped in fives, and have a reddish-brown bark. Trunks can grow to almost 7 feet in diameter, and mature trees sport very crooked branches.

Ponderosa Pine

Jeffrey Pine

Pines found at higher elevations include the lodgepole and white-bark. The **lodgepole pine,** the most widely distributed pine in North America, groups its needles in twos; it has yellow-orange bark and small cones. The **whitebark pine** bunches five needles together and has sticky purple-tinted cones. These pines tend to be smaller, and are found closer to the tree line.

Firs are another species of conifer found in the parks. **Red firs,** with short needles that curl up and cones ranging from 5 to 8 inches, are found at elevations of 6,000 to 9,000 feet. **White firs,** found at lower elevations from about 3,500 to 8,000 feet, have 2-inch needles that grow in twists off the branch, grayish bark, and 3- to 5-inch cones. Wildlife often take refuge in the large cavities near the base of old trunks. Both firs grow in forests near Yosemite's Glacier Point and in the high country along Tioga Road. White firs can be seen throughout Sequoia & Kings Canyon.

Sugar Pine

Lodgepole Pine

At the highest elevations (9,000–14,000 ft.), look for **foxtail pines,** gnarled trees that have adapted to the harsh rocky life of living at the top. This pine, like the whitebark pine, looks stunted and warped, often with a twisted trunk and spiky, dead-looking top. The roots grow over granite and require only a short growing season, allowing the tree to cling to a frigid existence.

Red Fir

White Fir

Foxtail Pine

The uncommon **California nutmeg** resembles a fir, with sharp single needles, and can be found along the Marble Fork Trail in Sequoia National Park as you near a creek flowing over marble slabs. **Incense cedar** is often confused with the giant sequoias, as both have reddish shaggy bark that almost crumbles to the touch. But an incense cedar has flat sprays of foliage that emit a fragrant smell in warm weather, and small reddish-brown cones resembling a duck's bill when opened.

The undisputed heavyweight of the national parks' flora is the **giant sequoia.** Smaller ones can be hard to identify, but there is no mistaking a mature 250-foot tree dating back 2,000 to 3,000 years. These trees grow to a height of 311 feet, weigh 2.7 million pounds, and can have a base 40 feet in diameter. Tree limbs can reach 8 feet in diameter. The trees are bare until about 100 to 150 feet up, and then sprout branches. The bark, naturally fire resistant, ranges from 4 to 24 inches thick. These trees resist decay and produce abundant small cones with hundreds of seeds the size of oatmeal flakes. Interestingly, it takes a fire to dry the cones out enough to release the seeds.

Incense Cedar

Giant Sequoia

   Giant sequoias can be found at elevations ranging from 5,000 to 7,500 feet, and occasionally as low as 3,500 feet. Obviously, the best place to see these trees is throughout Sequoia & Kings Canyon National Parks. The large stands of Giant Forest and Grant Grove offer fantastic, easily accessible examples of giant sequoias, and there are other groves, accessible by foot, scattered throughout the park. Yosemite has three stands of giant sequoias—the Mariposa Grove near Wawona, and the smaller Tuolumne and Merced groves near the Big Oak Flat Entrance.

   Broadleaf trees in the area include the **California black oak,** which grows at lower elevations in both parks. The dark gray to black bark of these trees is distinctive. They also produce acorns and can grow to a height of 75 feet. The **blue oak** loses its leaves in fall and can be found in foothills of elevation 1,000 to 5,000 feet. Hollylike evergreen leaves mark the **canyon live oak,** the other common oak tree in the region.

   The **Pacific dogwood** produces blooms with whitish-green flowers each spring. The **quaking aspen** has paper-thin white bark and an army of small leaves that rustle in the slightest wind. Along streams and rivers at lower elevations, look for cottonwoods, willows, and alders.

Canyon Live Oak

Wildflowers produce an array of colors during spring and summer, as they peek from cracks and crevices or carpet fields and meadows. The blooming season begins in February in the lowlands, lasting into early fall in the high country. The list of wildflowers found in these parks is intimidating and includes more than 50 species, some of which are described below.

Splashed on meadows and along hillsides is a lavender flower, **lupine.** It's easily recognized by its palmate leaves—leaves that originate from a central point like fingers from a hand. Look for the bloom along valley floors and in the Wawona region of Yosemite. You will also see **cow parsnip** here, bluish-tinged flowers set on spindly stems, with almost fernlike leaves. The cow parsnip's dartlike flowers resemble violets at a distance, but closer inspection reveals an umbrella-shaped top and leafless stalk. Large blue-to-purple blooms that shoot out amid tall, narrow leaves are **wild irises.** In the Wawona region of Yosemite, look for **mountain misery,** clumps of small, white flowers atop fluffy, pine-needle-looking leaves; and **farewell-to-spring,** a whimsical pinkish flower with four large, fragile petals and small, slender leaves.

Lupine

Cow Parsnip

You may also see monkey flower, showy milkweed, and yarrow at these elevations. The **monkey flower** is one of nature's brightest flowers, ranging from blue to purple, pink, and orange, and seen along streams and at high altitudes in gravelly soil. Petals consist of two-lipped blossoms that more imaginative folk say resemble the smiling face of a monkey. The **showy milkweed** grows in meadows and forest clearings. These sturdy plants have large oval-shaped leaves and stalks filled with a poisonous milky sap. In summer, colorful bunches of tiny five-petal flowers appear; later the milkweed pods burst, releasing a tuft of silky seeds to scatter in the wind. Growing up to 3 feet tall, **yarrow** blooms as a flat, wide cluster of white (occasionally pink) flowers with a pungent aroma. It was used by Native Americans as a healing herb, a drink to cure indigestion and to reduce fever. Today, the dried flower is commonly seen in potpourri.

Yarrow

Monkey Flower

At night, look for **evening primrose**—its four-petal flowers open at sunset and wilt in the morning, and are pollinated by moths. Blossoms range from white to yellow and pink and have a sweet lemon smell; stems can reach 6 feet.

One of the last flowers of the season is **meadow goldenrod,** which appears in late summer and fall. The plant grows in long stalks, with narrow leaves protruding all along it, and may be topped by a shock of yellow that resembles a feather. Goldenrod was used by American Indians to cure all sorts of ailments.

Evening Primrose

Meadow Goldenrod

In forests, you'll find pussy paws and snow plant in the shade, and lupine, mariposa lily, and mountain violet in the sun. The **snow plant** has a flaming red or orange stalk, while **pussy paws** have small, fuzzy leaves and delicate flowers that group together to resemble the shape of a cat's paw. The **mariposa lily,** which blooms beneath pines in Yosemite, is named for the Spanish word for butterfly, which it is said to resemble. Blooms consist of three snow-white petals with dark spots at their base; the long stems give the flowers a floating appearance. American Indians roasted the bulbs of these blooms to eat.

Mariposa Lily

At higher and cooler elevations, a number of slender blooms abound. The **mountain sorrel** has leaves shaped like lilies, with clusters of small pink flowers no bigger than the tip of a fingernail. The **spreading phlox** has pointed leaves that stick out like thorns and broad, flat flowers on top. The **meadow penstemon** produces a group of bright pink flowers atop a single, slender stalk. The blooms are arranged like trumpets, pointing in every direction.

Meadow Penstemon

Mountain Sorrel

A favorite flower of hummingbirds, **columbine** grows in meadows and springs from rocky crevices. It looks quite fragile, with bushy leaves clumped at the base of bare stalks that produce droopy blooms. The color can vary, but look for five petals that extend backward in a long, pointed tube.

Columbine

SHRUBS & PLANTS

One of the many plants found in the parks is the wild azalea. These plants resemble their household cousins and are often the first to proclaim the arrival of spring, with an abundance of vibrant color. The Sierra sports just one variety: the **western azalea,** a low-lying shrub with smooth, deep-green leaves.

Western Azalea

Bear clover is a low-growing shrub with sticky leaves and a pungent smell, found in the Lodgepole area of Sequoia and at elevations around 7,000 to 8,000 feet.

The **mariposa manzanita,** with its smooth red-to-purple bark and oval, coin-size leaves, blooms year-round and is but one type of manzanita common in this region. The mariposa manzanita produces small white and pink clusters of flowers that eventually turn into berries that look like little apples, which is what *manzanita* means in Spanish. This shrub is plentiful in the foothills of Sequoia National Park.

Mariposa Manzanita

Now look up into oak trees and search for a clump of green bush that looks as if it were growing out of branches. This is **mistletoe.** Despite its holiday charm, it is a parasite more than a shrub, growing in green bunches high up in the treetops and sucking nourishment from oaks and other trees. Another pest is **poison oak,** prevalent below 5,000 feet. Watch for a shrub with shiny three-leaf clusters and white berries. In winter, poison-oak stems are bare and very difficult to recognize, so steer clear of any thickets that resemble sticks stuck in the ground.

Poison Oak

3 THE FAUNA

Think of the parks as nature's zoo. There are no cages, no man-made habitats—just wide-open spaces with enough room for more than 200 species of mammals and birds, some of which are described below.

BIRDS

The Sierra Nevada is a bird-watcher's paradise. Each year, 135 species visit Yosemite Valley alone. The most treasured of the area's feathered friends include the great horned owl, the peregrine falcon, and the California condor, all of which send bird-watchers into ornithological ecstasy.

You're more likely to hear the **great horned owl** than see one. Its hoots sound like sonar, but since it is nocturnal, it's difficult to spot. If you happen to hear it, try to locate its branch first, and then the bird: It has large tufts of feathers near both ears. But don't get disheartened if you search in vain—these birds are great ventriloquists. You'll have more luck observing a pair of nesting **peregrine falcons** on El Capitan or Glacier Point, although you'll need binoculars. For several years now, a number of pairs have made this their own personal day-care center, hatching and raising their young on narrow ledges before beginning flight instruction. One of four falcon species in the park, the peregrine falcon is marked by a hood of dark feathers from head to back, contrasting against lighter ones underneath. This bird is a wizard in flight, reaching speeds of up to 200 mph mid-dive. It was recently removed from the endangered species list.

Peregrine Falcon

Great Horned Owl

Still endangered is the **California condor,** the largest land bird in North America, with a 9-foot wingspan. The birds are able to glide 10 miles at a time without flapping their wings. Keen eyesight allows them to spot a dead animal carcass from miles away. Their numbers dropped below 40 in 1975, due to pesticide use and the loss of habitat to building. A pair of condors can raise only one young every 2 years. In the 1980s, the remaining birds were captured and placed in zoos, where the young were hand-reared. Then some of the adolescent birds were released into the wild and have been seen occasionally in Kings Canyon. Today, about 300 California condors exist in the wild.

California Condor

In both Yosemite and Sequoia & Kings Canyon, the birds you're most likely to see are the American robin, Steller's jay, acorn woodpecker, northern flicker, band-tailed pigeon, two varieties of blackbird, sparrow, swift, American dipper, belted kingfisher, duck, warbler, brown creeper, mountain chickadee, and red-breasted and white-breasted nuthatches. Yosemite Valley is a great place to see many of these species because its environment includes streambeds, rivers, forest, and meadowlands, often within the space of a city block. A stroll anywhere along the Merced River should take you within visual distance of all of these birds, whose habitats include the water, meadows, and adjacent forests.

A reddish-orange breast easily distinguishes the **American robin.** These are the same birds you can see back home throughout much of North America, in suburbs and backyards, building cup-shaped nests on windowsills or the ledges of buildings. Before the bird adapted to urban living, it preferred a woodland habitat. It has long been considered a harbinger of spring, but in reality some of these birds stay put year-round. The **Steller's jay** is one of nature's more annoying birds. Unfazed by humans, it is a bold beggar, landing on picnic tables and elsewhere near food, while letting loose a screech that could wake the dead. The Steller's jay is bright blue, with a dark head and prominent crest. This bird is also capable of a beautiful soft warble.

American Robin

Steller's Jay

Like the Steller's jay, you're likely to hear the **woodpecker** before you see it—listen for its methodical rata-tat-tat. Woodpeckers can also emit a startling call that sounds like "wack-up." Woodpeckers are distinguished by black-and-white markings and a red crown, with an occasional bit of yellow. The **northern flicker** is also a woodpecker— look for a brown-feathered bird clinging to the side of a tree. Its wings have a reddish tinge and it sports a red mustache. This bird prefers to feed on the ground, where it searches for ants. **Band-tailed pigeons** are similar to their city-dwelling cousins but prefer tall forest trees to buildings.

Northern Flicker

Band-Tailed Pigeon

In meadowlands, you will likely see sparrows, the black-headed grosbeak, the uncommon western tanager—a bird with fluorescent feathers—and two varieties of blackbird. The **Brewer's blackbird** and the **red-winged blackbird** both make their home here. Brewer's blackbirds nest in trees, while their red-winged relatives prefer slightly marshy areas. Red-winged males have distinctive red patches on their wings. The Brewer's blackbird is, well, black, and females of either variety are drab in comparison to the males. **Sparrows** are small singing birds, streaked by brown feathers and with cone-shaped beaks. Their babies leave the nest 10 days after birth. The **black-headed grosbeak** has black, white, and orange markings, and a distinctive beak used for cracking seeds. Its soft, lyrical warble is music compared to those of other valley dwellers, and this bird is considered a sure sign of spring. The easy-to-spot **western tanager** is bright yellow with a reddish-orange head and is frequently observed in Yosemite Valley during spring and summer.

Brewer's Blackbird

Black-Headed Grosbeak

Western Tanager

If you're near moving water, you might search for American dippers, belted kingfishers, ducks, and warblers. The **American dipper** is notable more for its flying acrobatics than for its nondescript color. The bird flies headfirst into the river to walk upstream along the bottom, clinging to rocks in its search for food. The **belted kingfisher** is a highly visible blue bird that flies low over water in search of prey. You may see it perched above the water, clinging to branches and underbrush, and keeping a watchful eye out for insects and fish. It has a reddish band on its chest and a noticeable crest up top. The call of the kingfisher is distinctive: loud, rattling, and clicking. **Warblers** are often called the butterflies of the bird world. They are small, brightly colored, and move with gravity-defying ease. Contrary to their name, warblers are undistinguished singers, but they're great at collecting insects.

American
Dipper

Belted
Kingfisher

In the forests live brown creepers, mountain chickadees, and red- and white-breasted nuthatches. The **brown creeper** is difficult to spot because of the camouflage feathers that disguise it among tree trunks. Small, with a slender, curved beak, the creeper usually begins foraging for insects at the base of a tree and works its way up, clinging to the bark with razor-sharp claws. The **mountain chickadee** is another songbird with a delightful melody that sounds like "chickadee-dee-dee." These tiny, friendly, hyperactive birds have dark caps and bibs, a gray or brown back, and a distinctive white eyebrow. They nest in woodpecker holes or other small tree holes. **Nuthatches** are the birds you'll see walking headfirst down a tree trunk—no simple feat. Also called upside-down birds, the red-breasted and white-breasted versions are aptly described by their names. They are partial to abandoned woodpecker holes.

And let's not forget the **swift,** almost always found in flight above Yosemite Valley. These birds spend more time air-bound than any other land bird. When they do stop, they cling to vertical surfaces because their tiny feet are unsuitable for perches. Look up to see swifts flying between Yosemite's great granite walls. Both sexes look alike, and colors run from drab grays and browns to black and white.

Brown Creeper

Mountain Chickadee

Nuthatch

In the Wawona region south of Yosemite Valley, you'll find the bushtit and wrentit, scrub jay, California thrasher, yellow warbler, lesser goldfinch, barn swallow, and ash-throated and rare willow flycatchers. The **yellow warbler** is the more colorful version of the warbler described above. **Swallows** are streamlined-looking birds with long, pointed wings. Swift in flight, they eat and drink on the fly. All are migratory, and some travel thousands of miles to the Tropics each winter. **Flycatchers** are better known for their insect-hunting abilities than for distinctive markings. The **willow flycatcher** is a threatened species and has gray, brown, and olive plumage. All flycatchers are very territorial. **Goldfinches,** sometimes referred to as wild canaries, are gregarious birds, with bright colors and cheerful songs.

Yellow Warbler

Willow Flycatcher

Bushtits spend most of the year in flocks of about 20, constantly twittering at each other with a soft, lisping call. These acrobatic fliers are small, grayish birds with tiny bills. **Wrentits** are secretive birds—hard to see but easy to hear. They seldom venture far from home and prefer to live in chaparral or scrub thickets. Once mated, they form devoted pairs, constantly pruning and preening each other. When seen close together, they resemble a single ball of gray fluff. The **California thrasher** is one of several thrasher species, all of which have long tails and nest in low thickets. They forage on the ground and are accomplished singers, though not as notable as their distant cousins, the mockingbird and catbird.

Bushtit

Wrentit

The high country of Yosemite and Sequoia & Kings Canyon attracts dozens more birds, drawn by altitude and mountain meadows, including the dark-eyed junco, kestrel, red-tailed hawk, killdeer, Williamson's sapsucker, Clark's nutcracker, and ptarmigan.

Juncos, often referred to as snowbirds, are common visitors to bird feeders. Small and friendly, these birds resemble the sparrow, which also frequents this region. But the dark-eyed junco has a pink bill, white-to-bluish underbelly, and dark feathers from the crown down its back, and can usually be seen hopping along the ground in search of food. The **kestrel** is the smallest species of falcon. Like the falcon, it kills prey with a sharp bite to the neck, as opposed to hawks, which kill with their sharp claws. The **red-tailed hawk,** equipped with broad, rounded wings and a fan-shaped tail, soars effortlessly, using its keen eyesight to scan the area below for prey. The **killdeer**— named for its shrill call, is a performer, often feigning a broken wing to ward intruders off when they venture too near its nest. And no wonder—nests are little more than a shallow depression in the ground lined with pebbles. Adult killdeer have two black bands across their throats, while chicks have one.

Junco

Killdeer

Sapsuckers are specialized woodpeckers that extract the sap from trees with their brush-tipped tongues after drilling holes with their beaks. They also eat insects attracted to the sap. The **Williamson's sapsucker** strongly resembles the northern flicker described above, minus the red mustache. **Nutcrackers** are bold cousins of the crow family. **Clark's nutcrackers** specialize in prying seeds from pine cones and make forests their stamping grounds. In late summer and fall, the birds begin hoarding seeds for winter, tucking them in a pouch under their tongue during transport to slopes, where they poke holes in the ground and bury their treasure. A single nutcracker can hide 30,000 seeds. More remarkable is the fact that they remember where the stock is buried by the position of nearby landmarks, even when the ground is covered with snow. Clark's nutcracker resembles a crow, with a gray head and body and black wings tipped with white.

Finally, the **ptarmigan** is a unique bird, well adapted to changing seasons in cold climates. These small, stocky grouse have mottled brown feathers in summer to help camouflage them against the rocky mountaintops where they live, but the feathers turn pure white in winter to match the snow. Like all grouse, ptarmigans have feathered legs, and in winter their feet are also covered with feathers. During the spring mating season, males sport a vibrant red comb and strut in short flights while cackling, all to attract a mate.

Clark's Nutcracker

Williamson's Sapsucker

Ptarmigan

In addition to the above birds, Hammond's flycatcher, Cassin's finch, common flicker, pine sparrow, chipping sparrow, white-crowned sparrow, and violet-green swallow are all prevalent in the high country.

MAMMALS

Mammals in these parks are not seen as often as birds, but for some reason they're a lot more fun to spot. Most common are the mule deer, raccoon, squirrel, chipmunk, fox, coyote, and black bear. At higher elevations, you may also see Belding ground squirrels and Douglas's squirrels, yellow-bellied marmots, pikas, pine martens, badgers, mountain lions, bobcats, porcupines, long-tailed weasels, striped and spotted skunks, and northern water shrew.

Mule deer are most frequently spotted grazing in meadows at dawn and dusk. Although they seem gentle enough, mule deer should be treated with the same reverence accorded any wild animal: Give them a wide berth and, of course, refrain from feeding them. Many injuries have been recorded against humans who attempt to get close or feed them. The mule deer is named for its large, mulelike ears, and adults can weigh up to 200 pounds, surviving on a mix of grasses, leaves, tender twigs, and herbs. Males grow antlers for use during the mating season. And no, it is not true that the age of a male deer can be gauged by counting the points on its antlers.

Mule Deer

A variety of members of the squirrel family reside in this region, including chipmunks and marmots. The most common is the **California gray squirrel,** often seen in trees with its gray coat and bushy tail. The **California ground squirrel** is a brown animal with white speckles that prefers living in burrows. The **Sierra chickaree** is a reddish-colored tree squirrel that chews on pine cones and frequently makes a squeaking noise. **Douglas's squirrel,** common in Sequoia, is an olive-to-rust or gray color, with a reddish underbelly. At higher elevations, the **Belding ground squirrel** is most easily distinguished when it's seated—its erect posture resembles a stake driven into the ground. There are at least five different varieties of **chipmunks** in this region. Smaller than squirrels, they're quick and love to chatter, especially when scolding those who venture too near. Chipmunks range in color from reddish-brown to brownish-gray, and all varieties have four stripes running the length of their backs. At higher elevations, you'll find the **yellow-bellied marmot.** Resembling woodchucks, they regularly sunbathe and can tease visitors into believing they are tame. They're not. Adult marmots appear yellowish-brown, weigh up to 5 pounds, reach 15 to 18 inches in length, emit a high-pitched shrill as a warning, and live beneath rock piles or tree roots.

Douglas's Squirrel

Chipmunk

Yellow-Bellied Marmot

The **porcupine** is a unique rodent. These short, stock-legged creatures are covered from head to toe with quills that detach at the touch, piercing whoever or whatever touches them. Each animal carries about 30,000 quills that serve as a serious deterrent to all but the stupidest predators. Porcupines sleep during the day and forage at night, curling into a ball when approached by a would-be predator. In spring, females produce one offspring, which is born with soft quills (thankfully) that harden within minutes. **Pikas** look like a cross between a rodent and a hare, and actually are distant relatives of the rabbit family. Pikas have oversize ears, although they're proportionately much smaller than those found on their cousins, and live in colonies above the tree line throughout the West. They scamper over rocks and emit a high-pitched squeal whenever a predator is sighted.

Porcupine

Pika

Raccoons are considered pests in suburbia, but in the wild they are shy nocturnal animals, easily spotted by their ringed tail and the appearance of a black mask across their eyes. Some are no bigger than a large house cat, but males can grow to be 3 feet in length and may weigh more than 40 pounds. These animals are adaptive, eating everything from fish and small rodents to fruit, nuts, and earthworms.

Raccoon

The parks contain a large number of weasel-family members, including badgers, martens, skunks, and what most people know as weasels. The **long-tailed weasel** can reach 16 inches in length. Usually brown with a white underbelly, in winter it can turn all white, while retaining a black tip to its tail. The badger and marten are distant cousins of the weasel. **Badgers** can reach up to 2 feet in length and weigh up to 25 pounds. This heavy, short-legged animal has black feet, black-and-white face markings, and coarse yellowish-gray fur. The **pine marten** is a fast, agile climber preferring high mountain forests. It is sometimes mistaken for a squirrel as it bounds from limb to limb, probably chasing a red squirrel, its favorite dinner. If you're not familiar with skunks, consider yourself fortunate. Best known for the awful scent they release when scared or under attack, skunks are otherwise cute, fluffy animals with distinctive black-and-white markings. Most common is the **striped skunk,** its white-on-black stripe running from nose to tail tip. The **spotted skunk** is rarer, but lives in Sequoia & Kings Canyon National Parks.

Striped Skunk

Badger

Foxes, coyotes, black bears, bobcats, and mountain lions also inhabit this region. Most avoid crowds and shun humans, but coyotes and black bears are frequently spotted in the middle of Yosemite Valley, where they rely on the misguided benevolence of humans who feed them. **Coyotes** resemble dogs, with long gray fur and bushy tails. They feed primarily on small rodents and the occasional fawn, and grow to weigh between 25 and 30 pounds. One of the coyote's most distinctive traits is its howl, a long, haunting call that some consider frightening. The **black bear** is the largest mammal in these parks. It is often confused with the grizzly bear, which is much larger and much more fearsome. Incidents involving black bears usually occur due to improper food storage. *Never* feed bears, and by no means should you walk toward them. Observe from a safe distance. Despite their names, black bears can also be brown, blond, and cinnamon colored. Adult black bears grow to 250 to 500 pounds, and larger ones have been recorded. They are omnivores, eating both meat and vegetation, and they've proved very adaptable to hot dogs, hamburgers, and cookies. Unfortunately, once they become dependent on human food, these bears can prove bold and determined to continue their new diet. At this point, they must be trapped and killed by park rangers. Therefore, you *must* follow food-storage regulations.

Coyote

Black Bear

Foxes, bobcats, and mountain lions are less frequently spotted in the parks, especially the latter two. The most common fox is the **gray fox,** with its bushy tail, reddish-gray coat, and black paws. Members of the dog family, they look larger than they actually are—average weight is 10 pounds. Foxes are skillful hunters and eat rodents, berries, rabbits, and insects. **Bobcats** inhabit Sequoia & Kings Canyon National Parks. They are nocturnal and resemble a large cat, with a black-spotted tawny coat. The "bob" refers to their stub of a tail, a feature shared with their close relative, the lynx. Adults max out at about 20 pounds, and while much smaller than the next predator on our list, bobcats can kill deer many times their size. They are masters of the slow hunt— methodical, solitary, and patient. **Mountain lions** shy away from any human contact, so seeing one is extremely rare. These large cats can reach 5 feet in length. Their fur ranges from tawny to gray, their tails tipped with black. Solitary predators who prefer elk and deer, in lean times they'll settle for a porcupine or skunk.

Gray Fox

Bobcat

Mountain Lion

4 THE ECOSYSTEM

Quite often, the ravages of nature are the forces of change, and such has been the case in these national parks. Recent rock slides and floods have reestablished nature's supremacy, and preservation efforts and long-term studies have been underway for more than a decade.

In Yosemite, the return of the peregrine falcon was heralded as a milestone. When bird-watchers counted three nesting pairs and five offspring in 1996, the news traveled across the nation.

Considerable attention is going toward restoring meadows, limiting trails, and bringing back native plants pushed out by the impact of humans. The valley has seen the reseeding of a black-oak forest along the bikeway between Yosemite Village and Yosemite Falls, while controversy regarding its future (as well as that of Hetch Hetchy) rages on.

Large boulders placed in the Merced River long ago by settlers and early park managers changed the course of the waterway and created unnatural swimming holes. These are being removed, and the river is being allowed to pursue its own direction. Volunteers are also working to repair damage done by hikers who step off the trails.

In Sequoia & Kings Canyon, fire management has been a major concern since the 1960s, when the park policies began to be questioned. Early on, tree preservation was the cornerstone of park policy, so natural wildfires were squelched whenever possible. But after a noticeable decline in tree germination, research determined that fire is necessary—it dries out the cones to release their seeds, burns underbrush, and clears openings in the canopy for sunlight to reach the seedlings. In 1968, an unprecedented fire-management program began that allows some natural wildfires to burn, sets prescribed burns, and suppresses unwanted blazes. Consequently, over the past 20 years, the increase in the regeneration rate of giant sequoias has been noticeable.

Other environmental concerns for the park include air quality and drought. Unfortunately, Sequoia & Kings Canyon is located near California's smoggy Central Valley, and thus has the most chronically polluted air of the parks in the American West, often obscuring what would otherwise be superlative views. In 2004, the Environmental Protection Agency designated Sequoia & Kings Canyon as an area in which ozone pollution was a risk to human health. Ozone pollution also weakens the trees, so that when natural drought comes along, these damaged trees often die.

Dealing with the issues facing Yosemite and Sequoia & Kings Canyon requires time, money, and commitment—all high hurdles. Partnerships have been formed with foundations, nature conservancies, and even oil companies to provide funding for study and restoration. But the single biggest issue for both parks remains overcrowding—they are too popular for their own good.

For most of the 20th century and into the 21st, the parks have walked a tenuous line between increasing visitation and consistent management of visitation. Research has changed some policies; experience is changing others; and educational efforts will, we hope, help preserve the parks for future generations of nature enthusiasts.

A NATURE GUIDE TO THE NATIONAL PARKS

9

THE ECOSYSTEM

Fast Facts

AREA CODES The area code for the Yosemite area is **209.** The area code in and around Sequoia & Kings Canyon is **559.**

AUTOMOBILE ORGANIZATIONS Motor clubs will supply maps, suggested routes, guidebooks, accident and bail-bond insurance, and emergency road service. **AAA** (℃ **800/222-4357;** www.aaa.com) is the major auto club in the U.S. If you belong to a motor club in your home country, inquire about AAA reciprocity before you leave. AAA also has a nationwide emergency road service phone number (℃ **800/ AAA-HELP** [222-4357]).

BUSINESS HOURS Stores are typically open from 8 or 9am until 7 or 8pm. Banks are generally open from 8 or 9am until 5 or 6pm.

DRINKING LAWS The legal age for purchase and consumption of alcoholic beverages is 21; proof of age is required and often requested at bars, nightclubs, and restaurants, so it's always a good idea to bring ID when you go out. Beer, wine, and liquor are sold in most grocery stores in California. Beer and wine are available in most restaurants; some have a full bar. Bars can legally stay open until 2am in California. Do not carry open containers of alcohol in your car or any public area that isn't zoned for alcohol consumption. The police can fine you on the spot. Don't even think about driving while intoxicated.

ELECTRICITY Like Canada, the U.S. uses 110–120 volts AC (60 cycles), compared to 220–240 volts AC (50 cycles) in most of Europe, Australia, and New Zealand. Downward converters that change 220–240 volts to 110–120 volts are difficult to find in the U.S., so bring one with you.

EMBASSIES & CONSULATES All embassies are located in the nation's capital, Washington, D.C. Some consulates are located in major U.S. cities, and most nations have a mission to the United Nations in New York City. If your country isn't listed below, call for directory information in Washington, D.C. (℃ **202/555-1212**) or check **www.embassy.org/embassies**.

The embassy of **Australia** is at 1601 Massachusetts Ave. NW, Washington, DC 20036 (℃ **202/797-3000;** www.usa.embassy.gov. au).

The embassy of **Canada** is at 501 Pennsylvania Ave. NW, Washington, DC 20001 (✆ **202/682-1740;** www.canadianembassy.org). Other Canadian consulates are in Buffalo (N.Y.), Detroit, Los Angeles, New York, and Seattle.

The embassy of **Ireland** is at 2234 Massachusetts Ave. NW, Washington, DC 20008 (✆ **202/462-3939;** www.irelandemb.org). Irish consulates are in Boston, Chicago, New York, San Francisco, and other cities. See the website for a complete listing.

The embassy of **New Zealand** is at 37 Observatory Circle NW, Washington, DC 20008 (✆ **202/328-4800;** www.nzembassy.com). New Zealand consulates are in Los Angeles, Salt Lake City, San Francisco, and Seattle.

The embassy of the **United Kingdom** is at 3100 Massachusetts Ave. NW, Washington, DC 20008 (✆ **202/588-7800;** www.britainusa.com). Other British consulates are in Atlanta, Boston, Chicago, Cleveland, Houston, Los Angeles, New York, San Francisco, and Seattle.

EMERGENCIES Call ✆ **911.**

GASOLINE (PETROL) Gas is expensive in and around the parks, usually about 50¢ to $1 per gallon more than in the more populated areas of California. At press time, gas was about $3 per gallon in the Sierra. Taxes are included in the printed price. One U.S. gallon equals 3.8 liters or .8 imperial gallons.

HOLIDAYS Banks, government offices, post offices, and many stores, restaurants, and museums are closed on the following legal national holidays: January 1 (New Year's Day), the third Monday in January (Martin Luther King, Jr., Day), the third Monday in February (Presidents' Day), the last Monday in May (Memorial Day), July 4 (Independence Day), the first Monday in September (Labor Day), the second Monday in October (Columbus Day), November 11 (Veterans Day/Armistice Day), the fourth Thursday in November (Thanksgiving Day), and December 25 (Christmas). The Tuesday after the first Monday in November is Election Day, a federal government holiday in presidential-election years (held every 4 years, and next in 2012).

For more information on holidays and special events, see "When to Go," in chapter 2.

HOSPITALS There are medical and dental clinics in Yosemite Valley near Yosemite Village. The **Yosemite Medical Clinic** can be reached at ✆ **209/372-4637.** The dental clinic is at ✆ **209/372-4200.** In Sequoia & Kings Canyon, the nearest medical facilities are located in the gateway towns of Fresno, Visalia, and Three Rivers.

INTERNET ACCESS   In Yosemite, there are a few spots in the valley—Degnan's Cafe, Yosemite Lodge, and Curry Village—where Wi-Fi is available free or for a nominal fee. In Sequoia & Kings Canyon, free Wi-Fi is available in Grant Grove Village and Wuksachi Lodge. Internet access is readily available in all of the gateway towns.

LAUNDROMATS   In Yosemite, there's a laundromat at Housekeeping Camp, close to Curry Village in Yosemite Valley. In Sequoia, there's a laundromat at the Lodgepole Market Center. In Kings Canyon, try the one at Cedar Grove Village.

LEGAL AID   If you are "pulled over" for a minor infraction (such as speeding), never attempt to pay the fine directly to a police officer; this could be construed as attempted bribery, a much more serious crime. Pay fines by mail or directly into the hands of the clerk of the court. If accused of a more serious offense, say and do nothing before consulting a lawyer. Here the burden is on the state to prove a person's guilt beyond a reasonable doubt, and everyone has the right to remain silent, whether he or she is suspected of a crime or actually arrested. Once arrested, a person can make one phone call to a party of his or her choice. International visitors should call their embassy or consulate.

MAIL   At press time, domestic postage rates were 28¢ for a postcard and 44¢ for a letter. For international mail, a first-class letter of up to 1 ounce costs 98¢ (75¢ to Canada and 79¢ to Mexico); a first-class postcard costs the same as a letter. For more information, go to **www.usps.com**.

PASSPORTS   See www.frommers.com/planning for information on how to obtain a passport. See "Embassies & Consulates," above, for whom to contact if you lose yours while traveling in the U.S. For other information, please contact the following agencies:

For Residents of Australia   Contact the **Australian Passport Information Service** (© **131-232;** www.passports.gov.au).

For Residents of Canada   Contact the central **Passport Office,** Department of Foreign Affairs and International Trade, Ottawa, ON K1A 0G3 (© **800/567-6868;** www.ppt.gc.ca).

For Residents of Ireland   Contact the **Passport Office,** Setanta Centre, Molesworth Street, Dublin 2 (© **01/671-1633;** www.irlgov.ie/iveagh).

For Residents of New Zealand   Contact the **Passports Office** at © **0800/225-050** in New Zealand or 04/474-8100, or log on to www.passports.govt.nz.

For Residents of the United Kingdom   Visit your nearest passport office, major post office, or travel agency, or contact the **United Kingdom Passport Service** (✆ **0870/521-0410;** www.ukpa.gov.uk).

For Residents of the United States   To find your regional passport office, either check the U.S. State Department website or call the **National Passport Information Center** (✆ **877/487-2778**) for automated information.

POLICE   Call ✆ **911.**

SMOKING   Smoking is banned in all public places in the parks.

TAXES   The U.S. has no value-added tax (VAT) or other indirect tax at the national level. Every state, county, and city may levy its own local tax on all purchases, including hotel and restaurant checks and airline tickets. These taxes will not appear on price tags. They total around 7% to 10% in the parks and the gateways.

TELEPHONES   Many convenience groceries and packaging services sell **prepaid calling cards** in denominations up to $50; for international visitors these can be the least expensive way to call home. Many public pay phones at airports now accept American Express, Master-Card, and Visa credit cards. **Local calls** made from pay phones in most locales cost either 25¢ or 35¢. Most long-distance and international calls can be dialed directly from any phone. **For calls within the United States and to Canada,** dial 1 followed by the area code and the seven-digit number. **For other international calls,** dial 011 followed by the country code, city code, and the number you are calling.

Calls to area codes **800, 888, 877,** and **866** are toll-free. However, calls to area codes **700** and **900** (chat lines, bulletin boards, "dating" services, and so on) can be very expensive—usually 95¢ to $3 or more per minute, and they sometimes have minimum charges that can run as high as $15 or more.

For **reversed-charge or collect calls,** and for person-to-person calls, dial the number 0 and then the area code and phone number; an operator will come on the line, and you should specify whether you are calling collect, person-to-person, or both. If your operator-assisted call is international, ask for the overseas operator.

For **local directory assistance** ("information"), dial 411; for long-distance information, dial 1, then the appropriate area code and 555-1212.

TIME   As with all of California, the parks are on **Pacific Standard Time (PST).** The continental United States is divided into **four time zones:** Eastern Standard Time (EST), Central Standard Time (CST), Mountain Standard Time (MST), and Pacific Standard Time (PST). Alaska and Hawaii have their own zones.

Daylight saving time is in effect from 1am on the second Sunday in March to 1am on the first Sunday in November, except in Arizona, Hawaii, the U.S. Virgin Islands, and Puerto Rico. Daylight saving time moves the clock 1 hour ahead of standard time.

TOILETS You will find public toilets at most roadside stops in the parks and all of the developed areas. They can also be found in hotel lobbies, bars, restaurants, and service stations.

VISAS For information about U.S. visas, go to **http://travel.state. gov** and click on "Visas." Or visit one of the following websites:

Australian citizens can obtain up-to-date visa information from the **U.S. Embassy Canberra,** Moonah Place, Yarralumla, ACT 2600 (© 02/6214-5600), or by checking the U.S. Diplomatic Mission's website at **http://usembassy-australia.state.gov/consular**.

British subjects can obtain up-to-date visa information by calling the **U.S. Embassy Visa Information Line** (© 0891/200-290) or by visiting the "Visas to the U.S." section of the American Embassy London's website at **www.usembassy.org.uk**.

Irish citizens can obtain up-to-date visa information through the **Embassy of the USA Dublin,** 42 Elgin Rd., Dublin 4, Ireland (© 353/1-668-8777), or by checking the "Visas to the U.S." section of **http://dublin.usembassy.gov**.

Citizens of **New Zealand** can obtain up-to-date visa information by contacting the **U.S. Embassy New Zealand,** 29 Fitzherbert Terrace, Thorndon, Wellington (© 644/472-2068), or visiting **http:// wellington.usembassy.gov**.

VISITOR INFORMATION If you're planning a visit to Yosemite National Park, you can get general information on accommodations, weather, and permits from the park's touch-tone phone menu at © 209/372-0200 or online at **www.nps.gov/yose**. The hearing-impaired can get information by calling © 209/372-4726. You can buy books and maps from the nonprofit **Yosemite Association,** P.O. Box 230, El Portal, CA 95318 (© 209/379-2646; www.yosemite. org). For information on much of the lodging within Yosemite National Park, contact concessionaire **DNC Parks & Resorts at Yosemite,** P.O. Box 578, Yosemite National Park, CA 95389 (© 801/559-5000; www.yosemitepark.com). Information on lodging and activities outside the park is available from the visitor centers and chambers of commerce in the park's surrounding cities. If you're coming from the west on CA 120, contact the **Tuolumne County Visitor Center** in Sonora (© 800/446-1333 or 209/533-4420; www.thegreatunfenced.com) or the **Yosemite Chamber of Commerce** in Groveland (© 800/449-9120 or 209/962-0429; www. groveland.org). On CA 140, contact the **Mariposa County Visitors**

Bureau (© 866/425-3366 or 209/966-7081; www.homeofyosemite. com). On CA 41, south of the park, call the **Yosemite Sierra Visitors Bureau** in Oakhurst (© 559/683-4636; www.yosemitethisyear. com). From Lee Vining on the park's eastern boundary, contact the **Lee Vining Chamber of Commerce** (© 760/647-6629; www. leevining.com). There's a **California Welcome Center** at 710 W. 16th St. in Merced (© 800/446-5353 or 209/384-7092; www. yosemite-gateway.org).

In Sequoia & Kings Canyon, start your search at the National Park Service website at **www.nps.gov/seki**, which provides the most up-to-date information on the park, lodging, hikes, regulations, and the best times to visit. Much of the same information, plus road conditions, is available by phone (© 559/565-3341). Lodging information is available from **DNC Parks & Resorts at Sequoia,** P.O. Box 89, Sequoia National Park, CA 93262 (© 866/807-3598 or 801/559-4930; www.visitsequoia.com), and **Sequoia–Kings Canyon Park Services Company,** P.O. Box 907, Kings Canyon National Park, CA 93633 (© 866/522-6966 or 559/335-5500; www.sequoia-kingscanyon. com). You can get a variety of books and maps from the **Sequoia Natural History Association,** 47050 Generals Hwy. #10, Three Rivers, CA 93271 (© 559/565-3759; www.sequoiahistory.org). For information on the gateway cities, contact the **Visalia Convention & Visitors Bureau,** P.O. Box 2734, Visalia, CA 93279 (© 559/334-0141; www.visitvisalia.org), and the **Sequoia Foothills Chamber of Commerce,** 42268 Sierra Dr., Three Rivers, CA 93271 (© 877/530-3300 or 559/561-3300; www.threerivers.com).

WATER   See "Health," in chapter 2.

INDEX

See also Accommodations and Restaurant indexes, below.

ACCOMMODATIONS

RESTAURANTS